Keith
YC Hung

Other publications by Longman Group Limited
on behalf of the Society of Education Officers:

County & Voluntary Schools
Educational Administration
Education & the Law
School Governors

Special education

Written by members of
the Society of Education Officers
and edited by Fred Adams

Councils and Education Press

Councils and Education Press Limited
(a division of Longman Group Limited)
Longman House
Burnt Mill Harlow,
Essex CM20 2JE

© Longman Group Limited, 1986.

First published 1986

British Library Cataloguing in Publication Data
Adams, Fred
    Special education.
    1. Exceptional children——Education——England
    I. Title
    371.9'0942   C3986.G7

    ISBN 0–900313–37–4

    ISBN 0–900313–75–7   Special Edition for College of Preceptors

Printed and bound in Great Britain by
Biddles Ltd, Guildford and King's Lynn

Contents

Foreword by Jackson Hall, President of the Society of Education
Officers 1985–86, and Director of Education, Sunderland.   vii

List of Contributors   ix

1 Background – before and after Warnock   1

2 The Education Act 1981 – exposition and implications   13

3 Assessments and statements   28

4 Appeals procedures   70

5 Integration   78

6 Post-sixteens and the transition from school to work   91

7 Health and other support services, and voluntary
   organizations   106

8 Teacher training and special education needs   123

9 Role of parents   134

10 Northern Ireland, Scotland and Wales   146

11 An international perspective   173

12 Conclusion – future needs and developments   189

Index   194

Foreword

The express purpose of the 1981 Education Act is 'to make provision with respect to children with special educational needs'. In fact, this Act embodied the recommendations of the Warnock Report (1978) and gave effect to policy and procedures which are markedly different from previous practice. It is estimated that approximately one in six pupils at any time and one in five children at some time during their school years require special education provision. The provisions of the 1981 Act are therefore very important for a substantial proportion – about 20 per cent – of the school population and for many families.

A glance at the chapter titles gives some indication of the scope of this book and its contributors have all been closely associated with the changes and developments ushered in by the 1981 Act. This book is therefore an authoritative and invaluable source of information and guidance about the intentions and operation of the 1981 Act for parents, members of education committees and governing bodies (of all, not just special, schools), teachers and other professional staff, inspectors and administrative officers, for students, and also for the general reader with an interest in the education service.

This book and the cause it serves and promotes merit a wide readership. I feel privileged to contribute this Foreword and, in commending the book to you, I wish on behalf of the Society of Education Officers to thank its contributors most warmly. The Society is indebted to them. I am sure that many others, for whom this book will be of use and interest, will also feel the same.

Jackson Hall
President
Society of Education Officers 1985–86
Director of Education
Sunderland

Contributors

General Editor

F. J. Adams, CBE | Former Director of Education, South Glamorgan
C. E. Brown | Deputy County Officer, South Eastern Education and Library Board, Northern Ireland
G. V. Cooke, CBE | Former Chief Education Officer, Lincolnshire
R. S. Johnson, CBE | Director of Education, Leeds
J. McLaughlin | Assistant Director of Education, Newcastle upon Tyne
M. More | Director of Education, Fife, Scotland
D. Rigby | Senior Education Officer, Buckinghamshire
C. Salisbury | Assistant Education Officer, Hampshire
B. Taylor | Chief Education Officer, Somerset
K. Tottman | Assistant Education Officer/Inspector, Wolverhampton
A. M. Webster | Assistant Education Officer, Cleveland
R. A. Williams | Principal Assistant Education Officer, Hertfordshire

In addition to the above, there are others unnamed who have contributed invaluable help and advice and to whom the Editor would like to express his sincere gratitude.

Acknowledgements

The publishers wish to thank Mr T Harding, former Headteacher, Condercum House School, Newcastle upon Tyne and Mrs H S Goodman, Head of the Hospital Teaching Service, Newcastle upon Tyne for permission to reproduce the chart on page 60, and The Child and Family Guidance Service, City of Newcastle upon Tyne, for permission to reproduce the chart on pages 68 and 69.

We are grateful to the Controller of Her Majesty's Stationery Office for permission to reproduce material from DES Circular 1/83. Annex 1 & 2.

Contributors

General Editor

F. J. Adams, CBE	Former Director of Education, South Glamorgan
C. E. Brown	Deputy County Officer, South Eastern Education and Library Board, Northern Ireland
G. V. Cooke, CBE	Former Chief Education Officer, Lincolnshire
R. S. Johnson, CBE	Director of Education, Leeds
J. McLaughlin	Assistant Director of Education, Newcastle upon Tyne
M. More	Director of Education, Fife, Scotland
D. Rigby	Senior Education Officer, Buckinghamshire
C. Salisbury	Assistant Education Officer, Hampshire
B. Taylor	Chief Education Officer, Somerset
K. Tottman	Assistant Education Officer/Inspector, Wolverhampton
A. M. Webster	Assistant Education Officer, Cleveland
R. A. Williams	Principal Assistant Education Officer, Hertfordshire

In addition to the above, there are others unnamed who have contributed invaluable help and advice and to whom the Editor would like to express his sincere gratitude.

Acknowledgements

The publishers wish to thank Mr T Harding, former Headteacher, Condercum House School, Newcastle upon Tyne and Mrs H S Goodman, Head of the Hospital Teaching Service, Newcastle upon Tyne for permission to reproduce the chart on page 60, and The Child and Family Guidance Service, City of Newcastle upon Tyne, for permission to reproduce the chart on pages 68 and 69.

We are grateful to the Controller of Her Majesty's Stationery Office for permission to reproduce material from DES Circular 1/83. Annex 1 & 2.

1 Background – before and after Warnock

Perhaps the most obvious and certainly the most important of all educational truisms is that every child is a unique individual with his own specific right to life, liberty and the pursuit of happiness, as well as his own obligations to and entitlements from the society of which he forms a part. In that respect, all children are 'special', and in pedagogic as well as parental and community terms all equally merit as much individual attention as their proper development requires. But not all children require the *same* amount of individual attention and indeed for many children too much individual attention can be positively harmful. Moreover, with the best will in the world, a community, however rich, has to set a limit somewhere on the amount of human, material and financial resources that it is prepared to devote to the education of its young people. Yet it is equally clear that some children (those with serious sensory, physical or mental handicaps or with very deprived home backgrounds are the most obvious examples) are more 'special' than others and will not be able fully to take part in and benefit from the kind of educational provision which is considered appropriate for the majority unless exceptional arrangements are made. So, for sound practical reasons, the public education service as it has developed has tended to distinguish between the majority of children whose needs are likely to be reasonably adequately catered for by a varied but essentially 'normal' educational diet, and the minority whose needs are so exceptional as to require very special provision either by way of special support programmes or in special units or in separate special institutions. 'Special education' is about giving exceptional consideration and providing exceptional opportunities and exceptional help to those whose needs (whether by reason of special gifts or, in the more generally accepted sense, significant handicaps, disorders or difficulties) are greatest, whilst at the same time acknowledging their entitlement to maximum participation in the social, political, cultural, moral and religious aspects of life which we all share.

[Historically, special education in the United Kingdom developed first in identifiable form by way of separate institutions to help the most obviously and severely handicapped, since this was (as it still is in the underdeveloped countries of the world) the most sensible way to proceed and to give some priority to special needs in the absence of an effective and sophisticated education service for all children. However, as the mainstream system developed and as special educational provision became more successful, sensitive and wide-ranging, the achievements of the system led inevitably to greater demands and higher expectations, and the balance of the argument shifted from considerations of quantity and availability to those of quality and appropriateness, with particular reference in recent years to the relative merits of 'separate' (special school and unit) and 'integrated' (mainstream) arrangements and the balance between the two.

The story of special education in the United Kingdom is surely one of which the nation has every right to be proud. If it is true (as many educationists would claim) that the mark of a civilized society is the care and concern which it shows for those of its children whose needs are greatest, the record of the United Kingdom in the development of special educational services will stand comparison with that of any other 'western' country, and British ideas and examples in this field have commanded – and still do – attention, admiration and imitation in many other countries. But things do not stand still in this or any other field of human endeavour, and the challenges of the future are as great in degree though very different in kind from those of the past. It is very clear now that public funds for services like education will be severely restricted for many years to come, but even if public funds were virtually limitless (as they sometimes seem to British eyes these days in the USA, Canada, Australia – and in some parts of the European Community) it would still be impossible to get things wholly and permanently right because knowledge, skills and insights are all limited and because special education (like all education) is always in pursuit of desirable but irreconcilable goals. Yet, in special education at any rate, if one looks back with an unprejudiced eye over the last 20, or 200, years there can be little doubt that, in terms of human happiness and individual fulfilment, real progress *has* been made. Of course, it is possible to argue (as some modern sociologists would) that the main drive behind the development of special educational provision has been the determination of the more privileged and advantaged in our society to protect their own interests by segregating the disadvantaged in order to ensure that they remain so. And no doubt many mainstream schools and teachers have over the years seen the development of separate provision for pupils with special educational needs as a necessary way of making their teaching tasks more manageable and protecting the interests of the majority of their children. Human motivation is seldom totally pure and unselfish, but it would surely require a peculiarly virulent form of prejudice to fail to identify within our special education system a great deal of caring concern, compassion and genuine humanitarianism.

The history of special education in Great Britain is clearly and elegantly described in chapter 2 of the Warnock Report.[1] The opening paragraph is worth quoting in full:

> 'Special education for the handicapped in Great Britain is of relatively recent origin. The very first schools for the blind and deaf were founded in the lifetime of Mozart; those for the physically handicapped awaited the Great Exhibition; day schools for the mentally handicapped and epileptic arrived with the motor car; whilst special provision for the delicate, maladjusted and speech impaired children is younger than living memory. Even so, the early institutions were nothing like the schools we know today, and they were available only to the few. As with ordinary education, education for the handicapped began with individual and charitable enterprise. There followed in time the intervention of government, first to support voluntary effort and make good deficiencies through state provision, and finally to create a national framework in which public and voluntary agencies could act in partnership to see that all children, whatever their disability, received a suitable education. The framework reached its present form only in this decade.' (ie the 1970s).

The 1944 Education Act placed special education for handicapped pupils firmly within the general duty of LEAs to provide sufficient and appropriate primary and secondary education. It provided that all kinds of handicapped pupils, except those considered 'ineducable' (a term later changed to 'unsuitable for education in school') would be ascertained by LEAs as requiring special educational treatment and that appropriate arrangements would be made to provide such treatment. It left to the Minister, acting under statutory regulations, the responsibility of defining the categories of handicap to which the formal ascertainment procedures would apply. Whereas the 1921 Education Act had provided for handicapped children to be educated only in special schools or special classes, the 1944 Education Act envisaged that less seriously handicapped children might be catered for in ordinary schools, although those with serious disabilities would, wherever practicable, continue to be educated in special schools. There were eleven (later reduced to ten) categories of handicap prescribed in the regulations: blind, partially sighted, deaf, partially deaf, delicate/diabetic, educational subnormal, epileptic, maladjusted, physically handicapped and children with speech defects. And there was a requirement that blind, deaf, epileptic, physically handicapped and aphasic children must be educated in special schools.

The 1950s and 1960s saw a very substantial and very impressive expansion of special educational provision. For various reasons (to do with postwar shortages and competing claims for limited resources) there was a totally understandable tendency to concentrate first on meeting the needs of those who had been, or clearly ought to be, 'ascertained'. Thus, over the years, special education came to see itself, and to be seen by the rest of the education service, as a separate world catering for that small proportion (about two per cent in all) of the child population who had been ascertained as handicapped and having for the most part relatively little contact with the mainstream of primary and secondary schools. The feeling of isolation was reinforced by the fact that many providers of special schools were voluntary organizations and that (largely because of the idiosyncracies of government building programme allocations in the 1950s) many residential special schools were established in adapted country houses remote from the urban populations they largely served. So, contrary to the apparent intentions of the authors of the 1944 Education Act and to the Ministry of Education guidelines which followed it, the narrower view of special education was underlined and the potential contribution of mainstream primary and secondary schools substantially underexploited.

In the later 1960s and early 1970s things changed considerably. In legislative terms, the most important development was the 1970 Education Act which for the first time brought all handicapped children, however serious their disability, within the framework of special education and imposed on LEAs a duty to provide education for all those children who had previously been ascertained as unsuitable for education in school and had thereby become the responsibility of the local health authorities. At the same time, as shortages eased and techniques improved and mainstream schools became more sensitively aware of the range and variety of individual needs,' there was a substantial growth not only in various forms of 'remedial' provision, but also in the number of special units and special classes (mainly for partially hearing and educationally subnormal pupils) developed within or attached to mainstream schools. Also (and this was as apparent in the USA, Canada, Australia and several West European countries as in the United Kingdom) the 'winds of change' were blowing in special education, and new ideas and new trends were emerging. Among the new (or sometimes refurbished older) ideas and trends, the most clearly identifiable were sixfold:

1. A growing understanding that handicapping conditions are much more widely spread, more varied and more complex than systems of categorization based largely on medical criteria tended to indicate.

2. Greater awareness that not only does the incidence of handicap and our recognition of it alter over time as a result of medical, economic and social changes, but also that the difficulties encountered by young people in their educational and general development are likely to arise as much from disadvantageous circumstances as from individual characteristics.

3. More general acceptance of the fact that parents, however much in some cases they may be 'part of the problem', not only have rights in relation to their children which must be respected but also have a unique and uniquely valuable contribution to make to their children's development which must be more effectively exploited by the professionals.

4. A growing recognition of the value, indeed in many cases the crucial importance, of very early intervention to help handicapped children and of the need for continuing attention with regular review and appropriate modification of support programmes to meet their changing needs.

5. A better appreciation of the fact that there is really no sharp divide between the 'handicapped' and the 'normal' but rather a range of *individual* needs across a continuum.

6. Wider understanding and acceptance of the fact that every young person has a right to as full, independent and 'normal' a life as possible and that therefore the aims of the community in relation to young people with more severe problems and difficulties must be as much 'integration' as possible into the 'mainstream' of school and community life.

These developing trends led a number of involved individuals and groups in the late 1960s to the view that what was now needed for special education was a radical review by an expert and prestigious special national committee across the whole field. There was also a feeling that, since virtually all the other major sectors of the education service had recently been or were currently being reviewed by national committees (Crowther, Newsom, Plowden, Robbins, James, and others), special education would never achieve the status within the system that it deserved unless it too had its own similar committee. So efforts were made to persuade government ministers and opposition leaders that such a committee was necessary. Eventually in November 1973, Mrs Margaret Thatcher, then Secretary of State for Education and Science, announced the establishment of a new national committee under Mrs (now Baroness) Mary Warnock's chairmanship to 'review the educational provision in England, Scotland and Wales for children and young people handicapped by disabilities of body or mind, taking account of the medical aspects of their needs, together with arrangements to prepare them for entry to employment; to consider the most effective use of resources for these purposes; and to make recommendations'. Within weeks there was a general election, the Conservatives lost power, and for several months Mrs Warnock was a chairman without a committee. Eventually, however, the Labour government gave the go ahead. The committee members were appointed during the summer of 1974 and the committee itself met for the first time in September of that year. It worked for three and a half years and its report was completed in March and published in May 1978.

The 'Warnock Committee' (as it was and is generally known, though it is necessary now to distinguish it from another and later 'Warnock Committee', chaired by Lady Warnock, which in 1984 produced a report of considerable significance on the problems of artificial insemination and genetic engineering) was a remarkable committee in a number of respects. First, it had a difficult birth – it took nearly a year and two governments of opposing political views to bring it into being (in the event, this was by no means all disadvantage in political terms). Second, its terms of reference were almost limitless in their implications, and hard decisions had to be taken about how far to go in certain directions. Third, it was a large committee (twenty-five members, plus fifteen additional members co-opted because of their special knowledge and experience onto subcommittees, plus ten government assessors, plus the secretariat). Fourth, it covered a very wide range of relevant interests – with a university philosophy don as chairman and a chief education officer as vice-chairman, its other members included men and women able to speak with authority for the universities and polytechnics; teacher training and further education; special schools and ordinary schools; LEA administrators, advisers, educational psychologists and careers guidance officers; parents; voluntary organizations and handicapped people; doctors and nurses; employers and trade unions; and social welfare services. Fifth as well as considering masses of evidence and reports, the committee and its subcommittees put a lot of time and effort into making visits and talking to people (including a considerable number of handicapped people and their parents) about the real problems of those actually involved in providing or using special educational services. Sixth, the Warnock Committee was a happy committee which, through all the long days of argument, only very occasionally (and mostly towards the end) exhibited signs of irritation and never became divided into identifiably opposed factions, even though there were differences of attitude, opinion and emphasis on a number of significant issues, as there were bound to be.

In the event, the Warnock Report was agreed unanimously without reservation by all the members of the committee. The report itself runs to nearly 400 pages and contains 224 recommendations. It represents the first attempt in the United Kingdom (and possibly in the world) to take a synoptic view of the whole field of special education and to present both a coherent philosophy and a blueprint for development for the rest of this century and beyond. The philosophy is not flawless (in one respect at least, 'pure' principle was deliberately modified to take account of hard realities) and to some extent the detailed recommendations have already been overtaken by the march of events. But the main thrust of the report remains as clear and as challenging as when it was first published.

The Warnock philosophy and recommendations for action were not 'plucked out of the air' but rather based firmly on what the committee recognized as right thinking and good practice in what they read and heard and saw. The essence of the philosophy can be expressed in half a dozen propositions.

1. The aims of education in terms of personal development and social involvement are *the same for all children* and all are equally entitled to what they need from the community to develop their potential to the full. (In a much quoted passage, the Warnock Report defined the goals of education as 'first, to enlarge a child's

knowledge, experience and imaginative understanding, and thus his awareness of moral values and capacity for enjoyment; and secondly to enable him to enter the world after formal education is over as an active participant in society and a responsible contributor to it, capable of achieving as much independence as possible').

2. While the goals are the same for all children, progress towards them is for some fast, easy and relatively trouble-free, while for others it is slow, difficult and painful and for a few the obstacles are so great that, even with the greatest possible help, they will not get very far.

3. Every child is a unique individual within a 'continuum of need'. There is no sharp divide between the handicapped and the non-handicapped.

4. Within the continuum of need, a substantial proportion of children – up to one in five at some stage during their school lives – are likely to require forms of specialist help, temporary or permanent, which are beyond the resources of most mainstream teachers in most mainstream schools.

5. The identification and assessment of special educational needs is a complex process which must take into account a variety of factors related both to the characteristics of the child and to his circumstances. Simplistic categorization and labelling can be misleading and dangerous.

6. Because children are all different and because they and their circumstances change over time there must be a wide, varied and flexible range of educational responses to meet their needs with provision for ongoing assessment and regular review.

From these propositions spring what may perhaps be called the three key principles of the Warnock Report, principles easy enough to express but infinitely difficult to translate into effective action. These are:

1. The only criterion of effective special educational provision is its effectiveness as a response to the needs of the individual child.

2. There must be maximum *integration* of all children with special educational needs into the mainstream of school and community life.

3. As the essential corollary of the second principle, there must be generous and sensitive *positive discrimination* in favour of those who have special needs.

Or to put it all in a sentence, special education is about *meeting individual needs* and involves *as much integration as possible* and *as much special help as necessary.*

The recommendations for action proposed by the Warnock Committee are summarized at the end of their report, and the summary itself takes up 29 pages. The recommendations cover every aspect of special education from pre-school to teacher training and research. It is interesting (and in the light of subsequent events to date, a little ironical) to note that the 'three areas of first priority' deliberately identified by the committee as most urgently needing attention were: provision for children under five; provision for young people over sixteen; and teacher training. There *has* been some progress in all three areas since Warnock, but in the case of children under five it has been pitifully small and in some respects negative, while in the other two areas progress, though significant, has been far less than the needs of the times demand. However, the Warnock Committee was always clear that the objectives it was setting would take a long time and a lot of effort and commitment to achieve. It was not to be expected that educational miracles would happen overnight.

When the Warnock Report was published in the spring of 1978, it gave rise to widespread discussion throughout the United Kingdom and indeed aroused considerable interest in many other countries of Europe and the English speaking world. Although some of the earliest press comments were predictably misleading, inaccurate and mutually contradictory, the general reaction on a more measured assessment from the press, politicians (of all parties), professionals, voluntary organizations and other interests involved was one of welcome and support. The report *was* criticized by a few voices, mainly on four counts: that the logic was flawed and the proposed new definitions too vague and imprecise; that the report dealt only with special educational needs and did not tackle the underlying social causes; that the report should have dealt also with gifted children; and (more seriously) that in a period of rapidly rising unemployment especially for the young and unqualified, it was wrong to assume that meaningful and satisfying *work* would be an attainable goal for the vast majority of young people with special educational needs, who instead should have an education directed towards preparing them for long-term (often lifetime) unemployment and 'leisure'. The first three criticisms may perhaps be quickly dismissed – the general message and intention are more important than satisfying logic and precise definition and in any case definitions can be changed if they cease to serve a useful purpose; the committee always knew (and said clearly in chapter 1, paragraph 2) that it could not go deeply into the *underlying* causes of educational handicap; and 'gifted' children were clearly excluded from its brief by the terms of reference provided when the committee was set up. But the fourth criticism was and remains more worrying – large scale youth unemployment has become the most dangerous and disturbing social evil of our time, and unless it can be tackled more effectively by government for young people as a whole, there is very little hope that the Warnock Report's intentions for young people with special educational needs will be realized and there is a grave risk that many, perhaps most of them, will languish at the end of the unemployment queue.

Soon after the Warnock Report was published the Labour government of the day (with Mrs Shirley Williams as Secretary of State for Education and Science) sanctioned a very wide-ranging and thorough consultation exercise. DES officials, clearly well prepared in advance, were quickly off the mark and in July 1978 a detailed eighteen-page consultative document[2] was issued covering the whole field of the committee's work. Replies were requested by the end of February 1979. By that time, the nation was in the throes of the 'winter of discontent' and just over two months later the Callaghan government was defeated at the polls and a new Conservative government under Mrs Margaret Thatcher took office.

The spring of 1979 was, for various reasons, not the most auspicious time to press for a major new initiative in education. However, the new Secretary of State, Mr Mark Carlisle, and the responsible Minister, Baroness Young, were disposed to be sympathetic, and DES officials and HMIs were strongly supportive. There was ample evidence of a very strong wish in educational circles and among many other interests that 'something significant should be done about Warnock'. The eventual outcome was a White Paper[3] published by the government in August 1980, setting out its approach and proposals for changes in the law. In general, the government endorsed the main arguments and emphases of Warnock, but by no means entirely. Unlike the United States federal government in its famous Public Law 94/142, it made no promise of substantial additional resources to promote and facilitate change. It was cautious about the under-fives, and it confined itself to very general exhortations about initial and in-service teacher training. In further education, it acknowledged 'the need to clarify the law in the interests of students with special educational needs' but said that this would have to await 'a wider review of the legal framework governing further education'. And it declared itself 'not at present convinced' that a new National Advisory Committee on Children with Special Educational Needs, on the lines recommended in the Warnock Report was really necessary.

When, therefore, a few months later, a Bill expressing the government's intentions was introduced into Parliament, it was given a favourable but by no means wildly enthusiastic welcome from politicians of all parties, from professional and voluntary organizations, and from the wider educational and community interests concerned. Opposition spokesmen in the House of Commons described it as 'Warnock without resources' or 'like Brighton pier' (OK as far as it went but not much use if you wanted to get to France!). But there was widespread recognition that the Bill as it stood was far better than no Bill at all, and that it would at the very least set the new scene and spell out the new rules of the game in legislative terms even though it left virtually everything else still to play for.

So, after one or two useful, minor changes had been made during its passage through Parliament, the Bill finally became law on 30 October 1981, as the 'Education Act, 1981', some three and a half years after the publication of the Warnock Report. The rest of this book is concerned with that Act, with the statutory regulations made under it and the government circulars of guidance issued in relation to it, and with their implications. There can be no doubt that, given a sufficient degree of understanding, effort and commitment, those implications could be enormously significant for the happiness and well-being of individuals, and for the health and reputation of our society. In the words of a later related report from a voluntary working party[4]: 'The Warnock Report and the 1981 Education Act have between them begun a process of change extending throughout and beyond the education service, which will be more profound and far-reaching than is yet commonly realized.' (That process) 'will continue well beyond the present decade, will affect the whole of the education service and all our children and young people, from pre-school to post-school, will call for the wholehearted cooperation of other services and other professions to a much greater extent than hitherto, and will need to generate new ideas, new attitudes and new practices if it is to realize its full potential.'

References

1. *Special Educational Needs*. Report of the Committee of Enquiry into the Education of Handicapped Children and Young People, Cmnd No. 7212, HMSO, May 1978
2. *Special Educational Needs*, DES/Welsh Office Consultative Document, July 1978
3. *Special Needs In.Education*. Cmnd No. 7996, Government White Paper presented to Parliament August 1980. HMSO
4. *A National Advisory Committee For Special Educational Needs*. Report of a Working Party appointed by the Voluntary Council for Handicapped Children, May 1984. VCHC

2 The Education Act 1981 – exposition and implications

1981

was a response to the w. report

The Education Act 1981, together with the Education (Special Educational Needs) Regulations 1983, constitutes the legislative response to the Warnock Report[1] and makes provision with respect to children with special educational needs. The Act received Royal Assent on 30 October 1981 and, although Section 14 concerned with special school closures came into force on 5 January 1982, the main body of the legislation was brought into force on 1 April 1983 by Education Act 1981 (Commencement No. 2) Order 1983[2].

The Act has abolished the categorization of handicapped pupils and has introduced the concept of 'special educational needs'. A child has 'special educational needs' if he has a learning difficulty which requires special educational provision. Learning difficulty exists if the child has (a) significantly greater difficulty in learning than the majority of this age or (b) a disability which either prevents or hinders him from making use of educational facilities of a kind generally provided in schools, within the area of the local authority concerned, for children of his age. Furthermore, any youngster aged under five years has a learning difficulty if he is, or would be if special educational provision were not made for him, likely to fall within either of these two groups when over the age of five years. A child should not be considered to have a learning difficulty solely because the language (or form of the language) used at any time at home is different from that in which he is taught at school.

Special educational provision is defined by the Act as any educational provision for a child under two years and that which is additional to or different from educational provision in schools maintained by the LEA for children over two years of age.

The concept of special educational needs established in this Act replaces the previous categories of handicap (educationally subnormal, maladjusted etc) and has removed authorities' specific duties in relation to dyslexia and autism which were previously included in the Chronically Sick and Disabled Persons Act 1970, Sections 25–27. The general notion of learning difficulty which is significantly greater than for the majority of similar age is not without problems of interpretation, particularly when seeking to help children with mild learning difficulty in the context of differences from area.to area, or even school to school, in the range of provision normally available. Considerations of significance of learning difficulty involve appraisal of a wide variety of factors as Circular 1/83[3] recognizes: 'The extent to which a learning difficulty hinders a child's development depends not only on the nature and severity of that difficulty, but also on the personal resources and attributes of the child, and on the help and support he receives at home and at school. A child's special educational needs are thus related to his abilities as well as his disabilities, and to the nature of his interaction with his environment.'

One of the more problematic areas under the new Act is deciding which pupils have, or might have, special educational needs at a level which requires the Education Authority to determine provision. The procedure of formal assessment is clearly laid down in the Act, (and is described also in chapter 3), but there are a great many pupils with additional needs who are being helped, and assessed from time to time, for whom the procedure of formal assessment is considered inappropriate. Usually many more children are involved in the ongoing *process* of assessment and guidance than are involved in the *procedure* of formal assessment. The point at which formal assessment under Section 5 of the Act is indicated will be determined by many factors, including local arrangements and provision and the views of parents and involved professionals; it is not an area in which precise guidelines or criteria will be meaningful for all cases.

The Circular suggests initiating formal procedures 'where there are *prima facie* grounds to suggest that a child's needs are such as to require provision additional to, or otherwise different from, the facilities and resources generally available in ordinary schools in the area under normal arrangements'. Certainly there is the expectation of formal assessment for all pupils in special schools, special units (except for reading centres and disruptive pupil units) and for pupils in mainstream schools with complex or severe learning difficulties. Invoking formal assessment procedures too readily will expose some families unnecessarily to a lengthy and perhaps anxiety-provoking exercise, and will tie down fairly scarce professional expertise. Very low levels of referral for formal assessment may lead to some children not receiving the additional help and resources they need; it may also mean that the LEA remains largely unaware of the new provision and practices it could be initiating to meet the special needs of pupils for whom it is responsible. There has to be some consideration of the significance and probable permanency of the child's special need, and the involvement of parents, teachers and others as appropriate prior to formal procedures is crucial to timely and suitable intervention.

When the period specified in the notice has expired, and having considered any representations or evidence submitted, the authority can decide to make an assessment and will then seek educational, medical, psychological and any other desirable and appropriate advice in an unprescribed form. In the event that a Statement of Special Needs is maintained subsequently by the authority, the professional advice on which the decision was made must be reproduced verbatim in the appendices to the statement.

Educational advice has to be sought from a qualified teacher or headteacher who has taught the child within the preceding eighteen months. In a great many cases this will involve the advice of teachers of a school age child being coordinated by the headteacher. Where for any reason a child has not been in school, educational advice must be sought from someone experienced in the teaching of children with special needs or who has other relevant knowledge. Educational advice on children thought to be hearing impaired or visually handicapped must follow consultation with a teacher additionally qualified to teach children with those handicaps.

Medical advice will be sought from a medical officer designated for this purpose by the District Health Authority. This person is responsible for coordinating all medical opinion (eg from a consultant paediatrician) and all paramedical opinion (eg from a physiotherapist) into a single piece of advice for the Education Authority. In requesting advice from the medical officer the Education Authority can require that he/she consult specified persons in the compilation of medical advice.

Psychological advice is to be sought from an educational psychologist employed or engaged by the LEA who must consult with any other psychologist whom it is believed has relevant knowledge of the child in question.

The Education Authority can request advice, but does not necessarily have to, from any other source as appropriate in addition to these three disciplines. The nursing officer and local Social Services Authority will already be aware of the assessment and *may* be the recipients of a specific enquiry. There is often the involvement of the Social Services Department in the families of handicapped children and it is difficult to see why the Act did not press harder at this point and require education authorities to obtain advice from that agency, particularly for children in the care of the local authority.

There is a very real shift in emphasis proposed in these sections on professional advice and the balance attaching to that advice. In the 1950s and 1960s an often crucial part was played by medical officers in assessment and subsequent placement. The 1970s saw a significant increase in the numbers of educational psychologists trained and working in education services; skirmishes ensued with regard to their role in Child Guidance Clinics (with consultant psychiatrists), their primacy in educational assessment (with school medical officers) and their part in determining provision (with administrators and advisers). In these terms, the profession of educational psychology made massive advances in the 1970s in hitherto almost forbidden territories. As noted by Cornwall and Spicer[4] in 1982, where the Special Education Summary Form (SE 4) was used under previous procedures (in roughly three quarters of the authorities in England and Wales) it was completed and signed by an educational psychologist in over 80 per cent of instances.

The balance of relationships and influence between professional groups shifts and is checked and shifts again continually, but in this respect the 1981 Act, Regulations and Circular had something quite clear to say about professional advice and advisers confining them-selves to their particular area of expertise. The Circular went a little further:

> Professional advice should not be influenced by considerations of the eventual school placement to be made for the child, since that is a matter to be determined by the LEA at a later stage. Because of this, any discussions individual advisers may have with parents about the child's needs should not be such as to commit the LEA, or to pre-empt their decisions about the provision and placement to be made for the child (Circular, Paragraph 35).

This is a potentially difficult area requiring discussion and clear understanding between those who advise and those whose task it is to determine and create provision for pupils with special needs within an authority. Interdisciplinary teams, particularly, might find themselves at the end of a lengthy assessment talking to parents who have been encouraged to play a part in the assessment and who wish, not unnaturally, to know exactly what is proposed for their child. The issue of special schooling is often uppermost in the parents' minds at this stage and advisers need to be able to give indications which fall short of totally committing the LEA but which go further than a list of possible and vague opinions. The new penumbral area between advice on need and the suggestion of type of provision, in addition to the realization that parents will have access to the advice, has added a dimension to professional report writing.

In the form that it comes to parents, a Statement of Special Educational Needs contains a brief account of needs and the various provisions and arrangements proposed, supported by a number of Appendices which are the professional advice and representations on behalf of the child from a variety of sources. This part of the legislation bears close resemblance to the recording of children thought to require special educational provision not generally available in ordinary schools, as outlined in paragraph 3.32 of the Warnock Report,

> Our proposed system of recording children as in need of special educational provision will differ from the present system of categorisation in several important ways. First, it will lay an obligation on a local education authority to make special education provision for any child judged to be in need of such provision on the basis of a profile of his needs prepared by a multi-professional team, whatever his particular disability. Secondly, it will not impose a single label of handicap on any child. Thirdly, it will embody a positive statement of the type of special provision required.

This has emerged quite strongly in the legislation and in the paper practice at least, in most education authorities since. The very next paragraph of the Report, however, fared less well:

> At the same time this system will be part of a much wider scheme designed to ensure that the individual needs of all those children – up to one in five – who require special educational provision at any time during their school career are appropriately assessed and met and that their parents are involved as fully as possible. We hope that this scheme, which is developed in the course of this report, will help to eliminate the notion of two types of children – the handicapped and the non-handicapped – both in theory and in practice.

That wider scheme, for Warnock, required the debunking of the distinction between remedial and special education and gave statutory expression to a fresh delineation which was much wider than the prevailing statutory concept. One might argue that the definition adopted in the Act (a significantly greater difficulty in learning than the majority etc) does not exclude this wider delineation, but the notion of one in five has not carried much conviction.

Where there is difficulty in ascertaining exactly the child's needs (or how best to meet them) from the advice, or where there is conflict in the advice submitted, a team meeting or case conference is indicated. The greater clarification or reconciliation achieved in this way is preferable to the difficulties which might well ensue from disparities between different sets of advice or between professional advice and statement of provision. Where such differences cannot be totally resolved, it is for the LEA, whose authorized officer will complete the draft statement, to determine the weight to attach to varying advice.

Where there is a clear indication that some detail within the proposed statement, or a statement of any sort, will be unacceptable to the parents, a meeting with the parents, probably with the relevant advisers present, is often desirable. Such a meeting would in no way be a substitute for, or alter the parental right to, a meeting with an officer within fifteen days of receiving a draft statement or the right to further meetings with any, or all, of the persons who provided advice.

Early and frank consultation with parents in these circumstances is preferable to the possible exacerbation of a sudden and unacceptable draft statement which can lead to the adoption of entrenched positions. Ongoing case work and meeting the special educational needs of pupils is rarely enhanced by mistrust, arguments and legal procedures. In these cases it is far preferable to use whatever flexibility there is in the Act at an early stage in an attempt not to have to use the legal framework later.

Administrators in education, perhaps with good reason, often have an ambivalent initial response to new legislation. In deciding on how to implement the procedures made necessary by the Act, a number weighed the possibility of being swamped in requests for lengthy assessment from vociferous minority groups seeking expensive extra provision to meet the hitherto unrecognized needs of their children. Others viewed with concern the problems arising from the potential decanting of handicapped pupils into unprepared mainstream schools. Everyone, and correctly as it happened, saw warm photocopiers and paper everywhere. This may have led to some very tight, paper-bound and nervous responses in some quarters and it is worth noting that very few parents of the handicapped go to the law if afforded honest and sensitive consultation with people who care about what happens to their child.

LEAs have made various arrangements with regard to which person or persons, actually draft statements. Whoever performs this important task, it is clear that the integrity of the advice received should be maintained and that the particular sort of productive tension which accrues from the disparity between perceived need and existing provision should be tolerated. In the context of no centrally-provided additional resources for the implementation of these new procedures, and bearing in mind the marked differences between authorities in their provision for special educational needs, it would be remarkable if these tensions did not arise. Nonetheless, the gap which sometimes exists between advice on child need and resource provision to meet that need is only highlighted by, and not the fault of, unfettered professional advice. At a time of economic restraint, the Education Act 1981 has given to the task of closing that particular gap a new edge which is keenly appreciated by those who draft statements and which should strengthen, not weaken, the partnership between parents and professionals. Major issues, like relationships with one's employer, the rights of children and advocacy, can become implicated at the point of significant disparity between expressed need and available provision, and debating those issues long and hard deflects attention; it does little to reduce the mismatch for the child in question. There is every good reason to debate those issues vigorously, particularly in a world of large bureaucracies, the sharp use of arbitrary power and the challenge to old allegiances. It simply does not usually improve the lot of the individual child and family when the general debate surrounds, and obfuscates, their particular predicament.

When making a statement under Section 7 (9) of the Act, the LEA is required to send a copy to the parents, to inform them of their right of appeal under Section 8 and to supply, in writing, the name of a person to whom the parent may apply for information and advice about the client's special educational needs.

The Circular expresses the hope that 'appeals will seldom prove necessary and that they will be seen only as a last resort'. The contact with professional advisers at the assessment stage, and the options to discuss the draft statement described in Section 7 (parts 4, 5, and 6) of the Act, ought to have given every opportunity to clear up misunderstandings and to make any necessary adjustments acceptable to the persons involved. The LEA may have already modified the statement in light of the parents' representations. However, any fundamental and irreconcilable differences of opinion about the special educational provision specified in the statement may become the matter of an appeal.

The constitution of appeal committees and the procedure for

hearing appeals under the 1981 Act is provided for in Schedule 2 of the 1980 Education Act and there is a general awareness that such a body may only confirm the special provision in the statement or remit the case to the LEA for reconsideration. However, appeals under the Education Act 1981 are likely to be a good deal more complex than those heard under Schedule 2 in the normal course of events. For example, details of the pupil's development and learning difficulty, or consideration of residential placement or the likelihood of parents presenting specialist advice in the form of a second opinion from other advisers are the sorts of features which indicate complexity.

The advice in the Code of Practice (from the Council or Tribunals) on 1981 Act appeals suggests that 'local education authorities should consider devising a *pro-forma* including guidance for parents which should be given to those parents who express dissatisfaction with the formal statement in accordance with Section 7 of the 1981 Act. This *pro-forma* should therefore give additional, clear guidance to parents on the "next stage" in the proceedings and should set out clearly their rights in respect of an appeal and should encourage them to attend any hearing if they wish to do so'. Such advice indicates the need to go some way further than a bald notice in writing of the right to appeal against the provision specified. As in so many areas, a great deal will depend on the interpretation and weight attached to guidance like this by officers of the local Council in their dealings with parents.

Parents are to be advised in writing of the decision of the appeal committee and what action, if any, the education authority proposes as a consequence. At the same time the parents should be informed of their right of appeal to the Secretary of State who may confirm or amend the provision specified in the statement, or may direct the LEA to cease to maintain the statement. Local appeals machinery is not involved where a parent wishes to appeal against the decision not to maintain a statement. In that situation also the LEA must notify the parents in writing of their right of appeal to the Secretary of State. It may be that where formal assessment has taken place, but it is not proposed to maintain a statement, the parent requests copies of the submitted advice. This need not necessarily relate to an appeal because a number of parents, delighted at the decision not to maintain a statement, may still wish to see what was written about their child. There is no legal obligation to provide copies of advice to parents in these circumstances and local practice will no doubt take account of the views of the professional advisers who supplied the advice. One might take the view that it is insensitive suddenly to cease to treat parents as equal partners and perhaps illogical to deny them access to papers which would have been theirs of right had a statement been required.

Initial responses to the Education Act were warm to the notion of the closer involvement of parents. During the 1970s a great many schemes, joint ventures and training programmes were devised and delivered as parental involvement became almost fashionable. The fact that parents were at least as interested in babysitters, transport, holidays, and what would happen when they (the parents) died, as teachers were in behaviour modification came as a shock in some quarters. The more confident and articulate parents were most noticeable in this respect but the points were no less refreshing or telling for that, and the disparities between groups of handicapped 'types' in this form of representation did not go unnoticed by professionals. Parents' views were, and are, the nearest thing, (but still not close) to a direct contribution from the children themselves that we have in this field, although we might do rather more listening to the children themselves where possible (Page and Clark, 1977)[5]. The status professions (paediatrics, psychology etc) were beginning to learn with regard to parents, in assessment and treatment, and the Warnock Report picked up and highlighted this desirable trend. The rights afforded by the 1981 Act (to make representation in writing, to see advice if a statement is maintained, and to appeal) fall a long way short of an adequate recognition of the central, substantial part which the rest of us must help the parents to play.

There is a requirement to review statements annually to ensure that the provision specified continues to be relevant to the child's needs. It is often the case that review is a school-based exercise with copies of progress reports on pupils being sent to the education office. In this way the appropriateness of the curriculum might be monitored and the review procedure could form an early warning device on the need for re-assessment. Where the schools' record keeping system and pupil profiling contributes to the annual review, and where the review is forwarded to the education office, there is a greater likelihood of improved surveillance of the continued appropriateness of a certain form of special educational provision.

Re-assessment may arise from annual review or in response to a request from the parent but must take place in any case on pupils between thirteen and a half and fourteen and a half years of age, unless the child has been assessed since the age of twelve and a half years. Pre-leaver re-assessment, as it is referred to in some quarters, applies to all pupils with statements and requires advice from the same disciplines as for initial formal assessment. Bearing in mind the numerous and rapid changes which are taking place in the area of special needs (fourteen to nineteen years), the changed patterns of education, training and employment (sixteen to nineteen years) and the increased involvement of other agencies like the MSC, this form of thorough reassessment is vital to planning a young person's next few years. The need for specialist courses for some at colleges and the need for carefully designed 'packages' for others through to nineteen years and beyond means that the requirement under the Act to reassess in the pre-leaver year is a useful and valuable part of the legislation. Reassessment at this age, particularly if done with an eye to the pupil's needs as a young adult, ought to lead eventually to a wider range of more flexible provision for students with special needs post-sixteen and to a more critical evaluation by special schools themselves of their achievements with such pupils to date.

The range of practice in LEAs with regard to students with special needs who are beyond statutory leaving age is extremely wide (see chapter 6). The extent to which some will accept the duty to provide even is uncertain, whilst others have many schemes in schools, colleges and in liaison with MSC. It is likely that through its rapidly developing schemes the Commission will increase its activity, and expertise, in the special needs area in the next few years. Working through its schools, colleges and careers service the special education section of the LEA could be influencing the content, quality and duration of post-sixteen training on a local basis. In this context statutory reassessment in pre-leaver year could form the basis for conferencing pupils with a view to the next four or five years.

At the other end of the age range (nought to five years) the 1981 Act has responded in a limited fashion to the views of the Warnock Committee. The 'named person', as described, has not survived in the legislation and the detail of support and advice from 'a comprehensive peripatetic teaching service which would cater, wherever possible, exclusively for children with disabilities or significant difficulties below school age' has not carried through. Increases in nursery education provision for *all* children and the provision of special classes and units for a small group of the most handicapped, as recommended, no doubt carried too great a financial implication. The Act confines itself in the main to the assessment procedure, links between education and health personnel and the involvement of voluntary agencies. At the request of parents, or with their consent, an Education Authority may make an assessment and maintain a statement in any form it feels appropriate with regard to children below the age of two years. The flexibility in this is most welcome and may well be seen as an obvious necessity by those who work in preschool services for children with special needs. The LEA must make some form of assessment on a child under the age of two years if the parent requests it. For any child under two years the term 'special educational provision' can be interpreted in a very general and flexible way also; the accompanying Circular (paragraph 66) points out that this can mean 'any kind of educational provision including support and advice to help parents to help their children'.

The local health authority is often the first agency to become aware of very young children with serious learning difficulty and must inform the parent where it is felt that a child has, or probably has, special educational needs. After affording the parent the opportunity to discuss this with an officer of the Area or District Health Authority, that opinion must be brought to the attention of the LEA and this applies quite broadly to the local Health Authority in the exercise of any of its functions in relation to children below the age of five years. The Health Authority must also inform the parent in the case where a particular voluntary organization may be of assistance.

One of the difficulties which may be encountered when specifying provision in a statement for a child between two and five years relates to the level of existing pre-school educational provision in the locality. For the very young child and his family, there is often a wide range of home-visiting schemes, play groups, mobile toy libraries and support groups. The specification of, for example, full-time normal nursery education with additional help for a three year old can, however, constitute a greater difficulty. In that LEAs are not under any duty to provide education generally for under-fives, and bearing in mind the disparities between authorities in pre-school provision, the matter of discharging the duty to provide for those with special needs (particularly in an integrated way) can become problematic. Special arrangements of a fairly expensive nature may be required to establish full-time nursery provision, with adequate levels of staffing, to cover the lunch period and to cater for the special demands made by handicapped young children. The demand is likely to grow from parents of young children with serious learning difficulties for pre-school education in 'normal' nursery schools and nursery classes. They will argue, with some justification, the desirability of normal models of behaviour and language for their children. The value of pre-school experience for the handicapped and the non-handicapped alike is well documented and LEAs may have to create new forms of nursery education to discharge their duties to children with special educational needs at this age.

Three main forms of integration were distinguished in the Warnock Report and one of the significant features to appear in the Education Act 1981 was the duty imposed on the LEA to secure education in ordinary schools for children with statements, under Section 7, given that certain conditions can be met. In recognition perhaps of the isolation from mainstream life which can occur for pupils in some special units within ordinary schools, the Act goes further (Section 2 (7)) and makes it the duty of those concerned to ensure that, wherever reasonably practicable, the child engages in the activities of the school together with children who do not have special educational needs. The duty to integrate has to take account of parental views, the child's needs, the efficient education of other pupils and should be compatible with the efficient use of resources (see chapter 5).

The appearance of these new duties in the Act quickened rather than initiated the movement toward more integrated provision, in that the emphasis given to this aspect in the Warnock Report really only reflected the early beginnings of existing new practice in LEAs in the mid 1970s. The Act has not precipitated the hasty transfer of many pupils from special to ordinary schools, as a few thought it might, and the picture is more one of LEAs gradually developing various types of mainstream provision as an alternative to separate schooling, particularly for those with sensory or physical handicap and mild learning difficulty. For any LEA with the resources and the conviction there are exciting challenges in the field of integrated provision and, if carefully planned, the benefits which accrue may reach out to include a wider group of people than just the pupils with special needs most directly involved. There is, as yet, no significant body of authoritative research on the effects of such integration but within the gradual process there are encouraging signs of new forms of intervention. The duty to integrate as detailed in Section 2 has greater implications for expenditure than any other part of the new Act and to pursue that duty vigorously and res-ponsibly indicates significant increases in, at least, specialist teachers and ancillary staff. Transport costs and minor building programmes might, in the long term, be the least expensive aspects. The LEA which is able to transfer or redeploy staff as a consequence of falling rolls or reorganization of services is in a fortunate situation but still faces the sizeable task of post-entry retraining. This will need to be achieved at a time when other changes to the initial training in special needs are proposed and when there are many demands on the time of teachers and trainers alike for in-service work such as management, microtechnology and new examinations (see chapter 8).

Section 2 of this Act, and the demands from parents for integrated education, will provide an impetus for local initiatives and for the more flexible use of specialist and peripatetic staff for some years to come. The transfer of staff from special to mainstream situations, which so often accompanies these local initiatives, can create anomalies in staffing structures and disparities in relative salaries. That sort of bone of contention between staff on the same school site assumes an importance for the acceptance and integration of the 'specialist staff', without which the chances of successfully integrating the pupils is diminished.

The general decline in the numbers of school age children in recent years and the trend toward reorganizing special educational provision, have led to the closure of some maintained special schools. Such action, even for the smallest of schools, requires the approval of the Secretary of State and requires the serving of written notice on parents, other LEAs with involved pupils and other interests, such as, for example, the professional associations. The notice has to specify the proposed closure date and must allow not less than two months for the submission of written objections, which the LEA will forward to the Secretary of State within a further month with any observations it wishes to make.

The closure of special schools can be a complex and controversial matter, not least because it raises parental anxiety about the continuity of education for handicapped pupils and may often involve the demise of residential schools. At times the logical and unavoidable action of one LEA in this respect can place another in a difficult position with regard to a small group of pupils for whom it has to create or modify provision of its own. In addition, the very length of the process (rarely less than eighteen months in all) heightens anxieties amongst pupils, parents and staff in schools where morale is especially vulnerable because the number on roll initially is often so low. There is a strong need for the earliest possible communication with other LEAs, for a programme of meetings and discussions with parents, staff and governors, and for the minimum delay in moving through the various stages of the procedure as outlined in Section 14 of the Act.

The Act, and the accompanying Circular, will have an effect in some places on the nature of relationships and the balance of 'power' between professional advisers, particularly over influencing decisions about provision and placement. In a more complex world of diversifying provision coupled with the design of individual 'packages' for children with special needs (against a background of developing new professions, economic restraint and possible litigation) the task of the responsible administrator will almost certainly become more demanding. Previous experience in special education, the support of a Committee prepared to discriminate positively in the direction of need and good relationships all round are the minimum requirements now to discharge even the limited duties of this new Act. Administrative bureaucracies tend toward generally applicable rules and blanket strategies, whereas the untidy exception and the one-off arrangement constitute the norm in special education; it is difficult to see how the new procedures will reduce the tension inherent in that.

Mention was made earlier of the influence of mainstream school arrangements, organization and attitudes on development in special educational provision and treatment in a local authority or area. In the longer term this may have as great a bearing on the type and quality of service to those with special needs as either the Warnock Report or the 1981 Act. The type, or types, of secondary and tertiary education decided upon, the commitment to pre-school provision generally and the ethos of mainstream schools will be major determinants in the evolution of new forms of intervention. Viewed alongside these considerable forces, the 1981 Act is of limited significance.

The legislation addressed itself to some of the less important features of the Warnock Report, like procedures of assessment, decategorization and parental involvement. None of these features was particularly gripping or new and in places the requirements of the Act, as with parental involvement for example, are minimal even in the light of existing reasonable practice. These aspects are, of course, inexpensive ones to attend to and most have managed to find a 'statementing officer', a psychologist or two and a few peripatetic specialists within the public expenditure plans announced by the Government at the beginning of the decade.

The three priority areas of the Warnock Report previously mentioned (pre-school, post-sixteen and teacher training) were not dealt with in any substantial way in the legislation. The expansion of provision, and increase in expenditure, resulting from statutory duties in those areas could not have been contemplated within existing financial limits. Any serious attempt to help the 'one-in-five' of the Warnock Report (or rather, the other 18 per cent) was never a realistic option in the financial climate of the early 1980s. This may be regarded as a cynical view of the criteria used for the selection of what to frame in law, but placatory and defensive noises about rearranging existing resources and developing different attitudes were much in evidence at the time, and the single potentially costly section, on integration, contains that interesting tail piece about compatibility with the efficient use of resources.

One or two major enquiries into how local authorities have implemented are now under way and it will be interesting to see how rigidly or freely the minimum requirements have been interpreted. A strict adherence to the letter of the law on its own is unlikely to foster the atmosphere in which new ideas and good practice flourish. If the previous deflection of legislative intent with regard to mainstream provision is to be avoided, and if a genuine attempt is to be made to enhance the development of roughly one in five children, additional resources will be needed, without which the benefits of favourable attitudes, good research and better assessment will appear like embrocation on a broken arm.

References

1. *Special Educational Needs*. Report of the Committee of Enquiry into the Education of Handicapped Children & Young People (The Warnock Report) HMSO 1978.
2. The Education Act 1981 (Commencement No 2) Order 1983, HMSO
3. *Assessments & Statements of Special Educational Needs*: Circular 1/83
4. *The Discovery & Assessment of Pupils with Special Educational Needs*, K F Cornwall & J C Spicer, occasional paper of the DECP, British Psychological Society 1982
5. *Who Cares? Young People In Care Speak Out*, R Page & G A Clark (Editors), National Childrens Bureau, 1977.

3 Assessments and statements

Introduction

After much uncertainty and speculation about the timing of the introduction of the new procedures relating to assessments and statements, the Secretary of State for Education and Science, Sir Keith Joseph, selected 1 April 1983 as the appointed day. Many cynics made suitable mumblings about the choice of date, while others welcomed the announcement of 10 January 1983 since practical steps could then be taken by LEAs, health authorities and Social Services Departments to prepare for what many were regarding the most significant part of the 1981 Act.

The formal statutory assessment procedures of the 1981 Act have replaced all the procedures set out in DES Circular 2/75 and the associated SE (Special Education) Forms 1–6. The SE Forms had themselves replaced the HP (Handicapped Pupils) Forms which were introduced in 1945. The principal difference between the new and the earlier procedures is that the 1981 Act procedures are mandatory and the statement which is their written culmination is a legal document, the provisions of which are binding on the LEA.

Identification

It is axiomatic that before a child who has, or may have, special educational needs can be assessed, those needs must be identified. Section 4 of the Act places upon LEAs a general duty to identify such children for whom they are responsible. This responsibility extends to children up to the age of nineteen years registered in schools maintained by the home and other LEAs, pupils in schools not maintained by the home or any other LEA, and providing due information has been given, pupils not falling within any of these categories including children who are not under the age of two years or over compulsory school age.

1981 Act.

Definition of assessment

An explanation of exactly what constitutes assessment is neatly summarized in paragraph 4 of Circular 1/83 in the following words.

The assessment of special educational needs is not an end in itself, but a means of arriving at a better understanding of a child's learning difficulties for the practical purposes of providing a guide to his education and a basis against which to monitor his progress. Whilst assessment should take account of provision, it is important that a clear distinction should be made in future between:

1. the analysis of the child's learning difficulties;

2. the specification of his special needs for different kinds of approaches, facilities or resources;

3. the determination of the special educational provision to meet these needs.

Paragraph 5 states succinctly that 'assessment is a continuous process', indeed, it can be no other since a child's needs will inevitably change as he grows older or as individual circumstances improve, deteriorate or simply alter, and these needs, therefore, should be under constant review, and monitoring by all those with whom he comes into contact.

The Warnock model of assessment

The Warnock Report devotes several sections of chapter 4 to assessment; paragraph 4.35 contains the recommendation 'that there should be five stages of assessment and that a child's special needs should be assessed at one or more of these stages as appropriate'. Warnock divides the five stages into two principal categories:

School-based stages of assessment: Stages 1–3. *See notes written*

Multi-professional assessment: Stages 4 and 5. *p. 230*

It is the latter two stages which have been subsumed into Section 5 of the 1981 Act. Good practice would always require that any child should be the subject of the Warnock model stages 1–3 before the formal assessments procedures are initiated.

Because of the importance of informal assessment it is important to examine how Warnock envisaged the first three stages. At stage 1 the headteacher in association with the class teacher or personal tutor, would collect all educational, medical, social and other relevant information about a child's performance in a school pertinent to his special educational needs, involving his parents wherever possible, and then decide how the school could best meet those needs. Progress would be monitored within school, advice from outside the school sought, if necessary, and appropriate records would, of course, be maintained. Stage 2 would be similar to stage 1 except that in addition the child's difficulties would be discussed with a teacher with training and expertise in special education. Stage 2 develops into stage 3 at the time when the headteacher decides to involve other professional staff either directly or with the help of the school doctor. Examples of such professionals could include a peripatetic teacher of the visually handicapped, an educational psychologist or appropriate staff from the Social Services or District Health Authority.

The Warnock model of assessment at stages 4 and 5 would involve all those from the earlier stages, but would seek the more specialist intervention of those with local or area responsibilities and those whose professional work provided them with a comprehensive overview of the various services and provision available to young people with special educational needs. Stage 4, for example, could include doctors, health visitors, educational or clinical psychologists, nursing officers, social workers, advisory or special needs support teachers likely to be involved and able to have the power of decision in relation to service delivery. Stage 5 would be similar to stage 4, but would be extended to include various staff with more specialist responsibilities often exercised over a geographically wide area. The concept of the district handicap team as described in the Court Report, with suitably expanded membership, would usually provide a comprehensive approach to multi-professional assessments. In some cases such assessments may be more regionally than locally based in recognition of either the low incidence, or complexity, or comparative rarity of a particular disability and the consequent need to concentrate resources into specialist assessment centres based either in an educational or hospital setting.

The coalescence of the Warnock five stages and the 1981 Act Section 5 models of assessment are depicted graphically in Appendix 3.1 together with its accompanying textual interpretation.

Parents as partners

The theme of parents as partners within the spirit of the 1981 Act can be no better demonstrated than in the implementation of Section 5 of the Act. It is hardly conceivable that parents would not have been closely involved in the SE procedures, but they now have the right in law to be consulted at every stage of the new assessment procedures. For some less fortunate parents this partnership with the LEA, the school and all the agencies involved in the potentially bureaucratic intricacies can be a distressing and confusing nightmare, while more articulate or alert parents will take full advantage of the new consultative processes and sometimes use them to try and achieve for their child a level and intensity of educational, medical or social provision which is beyond the resources of the authority to provide; this poses a dilemma. All parents are entitled to the same degree of involvement, the level of service which is right for their child and the sensitivity which human dignity demands in response to the difficulties often caused by a child with special educational needs both at home and elsewhere. Further reference is made later in the chapter to any potential discrepancies between the level of educational and other provision required by the child and that described in the statement.

The duty to assess

Subsection 5(1) states that LEAs shall make an assessment if they are of the opinion that a child for whom they are responsible has, or probably has, special educational needs which require that special educational provision should be made for him. In other words this is a duty imposed on LEAs by the Act once the child's needs have been identified.

The notice

The first step which the LEA must take, if it proposed to assess a child's educational needs, is to serve notice on the child's parents in accordance with Section 5(3), before any other action is taken. This written notice must contain the following four essential pieces of information:

1. the fact that the LEA is proposing to make an assessment;

2. the procedure which it will be following in making it;

3. the name of an officer of the LEA from whom further information may be obtained;

4. the parents' right to make representations, and submit written evidence to the LEA within a period of not less than 29 days from the date on which the notice was served.

This written notice should not be the first intimation to the parents of the LEA's proposal to make an assessment because of their child's learning difficulties. It is to be expected that informal assessment procedures will already have been completed before this stage is reached and the parents will presumably, therefore, know some of the professional staff who are likely to take part in the formal assessment.

The notice would normally be sent from the Education Department or Area Office and signed by an assistant education officer or assistant director of education.

In the case of children in care of the local authority, the notice should be sent to a designated officer in the Social Services Department with a copy to the child's parents or parent. Many LEAs have prepared an information booklet for parents to accompany the notice giving details of the procedures followed during the assessment and general information about the facilities and educational provision available to children and young people with special educational needs. In addition, parents should already have access to the booklets or leaflets which the LEA publishes annually setting out information about the services provided generally by the LEA and also by the District Health Authority and other local authority services.

The officer of the Education Department named in the notice should be one who has sufficient and relevant experience of the whole field of special education, of dealing with parents, members of the public, colleagues from the various parts of the education service and other local authority departments, health authorities and central government departments. Such a person must be able to inspire confidence in parents as he or she is likely to be the first person with whom parents will come into contact, either by telephone, in person or by letter, if information supplementary to the notice is being sought. The role which this officer plays cannot be emphasized too strongly, since he or she can colour the whole tenor of future relations between the parents and the LEA.

The representations which parents make in response to the notice may take a variety of forms; they may serve to reinforce the proposal to make the assessment, or indicate that the parent needs more information, or reassurances as to what might or could happen if the assessment goes ahead, reveal difficulties of which the LEA was unaware, or convince the LEA that it would not be in the child's best interests for the assessment to proceed either at that time or under existing circumstances.

The written evidence which parents are at liberty to submit could provide useful information about the child and his family, which will assist the whole assessment process. Depending on the particular aspect of the learning difficulty the evidence must, for example, relate to the child's medical condition, particularly difficult home circumstances which are affecting the child's general temperament or performance at school, or attitude or fears about some or all of his work at school. It is at times like this when many parents with every justification say to the officers of the LEA 'I know my child', and the situation is either very much better, very much worse or completely different from the image which they believe the LEA has of their child. Any officer who ignores or tries to dismiss such representations or evidence, whether written or oral, is taking a risk over the child's future welfare and the LEA's credibility.

Some parents may need assistance to enable them to understand and respond to the notice. If any show signs of bewilderment, they should be given every possible assistance by letter, telephone or in person either by home visits or visits to LEA offices. Any parents with language problems should have access to translations and interpreters. Any LEA officer who prepares a written response on the parents' behalf at their request must firstly ensure impartiality, and secondly that there is no conflict of interests. The written version of any information given orally must be agreed by the parents. Some parents may find an ally or friend in the local representatives of national organizations, eg MENCAP, MIND, RNIB, RNID. LEAs should actually suggest the name of a voluntary organization or an employee of a statutory body or the name of an LEA officer who would be able and willing to help. The parents of a child in care may wish to submit evidence or make representations to the LEA through the Social Services Department in response to the notice. When parents are separated or divorced, the notice should go to the parent who is looking after or has custody of the child; if the whereabouts of the other parent is known, a copy of the notice should usually be sent to him or her indicating the same right of reply. Experience has so far shown that it can be extremely difficult to trace such a parent and even if traceable he or she often remains silent.

The 29 day period in which parents may respond to the notice is significant only in as much as it is just short of one month but long enough for parents to reflect on and consider the impact of the substance of the notice. In practice experience has so far shown that parents do not require such a protracted period within which to respond, since many opt to reply by return of post and more often than not positively.

There was much debate in the early days of 1983 and even subsequently both within LEAs and by other agencies, about the way in which the notice was actually to be served on the parents. Suggestions varied from use of the normal postal service, recorded delivery or possibly even registered post. There were also suggestions that a communication of this nature should be hand delivered and discussion ensued as to who would be the best person; the most obvious choices were either the education welfare officer or the educational psychologist; the most important factor, however, is that whoever delivers the notice is conversant with the terms and procedures of the 1981 Act. Discretion is left to the LEA in the absence of any legal requirement.

Despite the fact that many parents respond positively within the 29 day period, parents are entitled in law to reverse or amend their initial response in the light of further reflection.

The notification

Section 5(4) states that if at the end of the 29 day period the LEA considers it appropriate, having taken account of any evidence or representations the parents have made, the educational needs of the child concerned shall be assessed. Section 5(5) stipulates that the LEA must write to the parents informing them of the decision to proceed with the formal assessment and of the reasons for making it. This second official communication between the LEA and the parents is known as the 'notification'. Copies of the notification must be sent to an officer in the Social Services Department, designated for this purpose, and the designated nursing officer in the District Health Authority.

If the LEA decides not to assess the special educational needs of the child at any time after serving the initial notice, the parents must be notified of this decision in writing in accordance with the provisions of Section 5(10).

Matters to be taken into account in making an assessment

Regulation 8 of The Education (Special Educational Needs) Regulations 1983 stipulates that the LEA must take the following matters into account when making an assessment:

1. any representations made by the child's parents (or legal guardian);

2. any evidence submitted by, or at the request of, that parent;

3. any written educational, medical or psychological advice or other written relevant advice from those qualified and competent to provide it in relation to the child's needs or ways of meeting them for the purpose of arriving at a satisfactory assessment. Examples could include advice from nursing, social services or education welfare officers;

4. any information relating to the health and welfare of the child furnished by or on behalf of:

   (i) any District Health Authority
   (ii) any Social Services Authority

Attention has already been drawn to the distinction between 'representations' and 'evidence'. There has been much discussion about the difference between 'advice' and 'information'. There is no doubt that at times the line of demarcation between the two is distinctly blurred, but one may broadly define 'advice' as recommendations for enhancing a child's progress through various forms of intervention, and 'information' as general details about a child's individual circumstances which will enable others to have a better understanding of the child's special needs.

Any person from whom advice is sought must be given a copy of any representations or evidence submitted by or on behalf of the parents; this would include a written version of any representations made by the parents.

The purpose of collecting the evidence is to enable the LEA to prepare a draft statement about the child's needs and ways of meeting them. More detailed comment on the statement itself appears later in this chapter. The method of collecting the evidence, like many other aspects of the assessment procedure, is decided at local level. Practices vary, although the more usual method is for the Local Authority Education Department to collect and collate the representations, advice and information, and then prepare the draft statement. Alternatively the schools' psychological service (also known in some authorities as the child and family guidance service) performs this function and prepares, agrees and even signs the draft and final versions of the statements. Another not uncommon model is for different parts of the formal assessment procedures to be shared between the Education Department and the schools' psychological service. In this model the mainly administrative procedures are carried out in the department, while the fieldwork elements and consultations with other professionals about the advice being submitted are the responsibility of the schools' psychological services. Many educational psychologists are sensitive to the fact that irrespective of where the balance of responsibility now lies within their own LEA for the overall assessment procedures the 1981 Act has introduced a wider sharing of responsibility than existed under the procedures for the SE or HP forms. The question of the signing of the statement is also dealt with in the later part of the chapter.

Advice

The advice sought from the various professionals forms a major part of the documentation on the child and, therefore, merits closer examination. DES Circular 1/83 states that 'the Secretary of State for Education and Science does not intend to prescribe the form in which professional advice should be presented'. This is a departure from the generally prescriptive format of SE and HP forms. Many professionals welcomed this flexibility, while others reflected on the desirable length of their submission, the style of language in which it was written, the selection of appropriate information, which would not cause offence to the recipient, particularly the child's parent, and the need to preserve confidentiality about the child's and his family's personal circumstances. Except in the more complex cases it transpires that most of what needs to be said can be summarized on two sides of A4 paper. In relation to advice from the various professionals, many LEAs have adopted a colour coding system, comparable to the SE and HP forms, which readily identified the different sources.

Suggested checklist

Although the format of presentation of advice has not been determined nationally, DES Circular 1/83, Annex 1 (see Appendix 3.2) contains a suggested checklist which is very useful and helpful. The checklist is in three main parts:

1. description of child's functioning,
2. aims of provision,
3. facilities and resources,

each with several sub-headings and specific points on which comment might be provided. The checklist provides individual professionals with the opportunity of selecting those points which are relevant to their own specialisms or to the circumstances of particular cases, or enables them to highlight issues which require greater emphasis.

There is no stipulation in the regulations that the advice must be sought in a particular order, although it is logical that the sequence should be educational, medical, psychological and other advice.

Educational advice

The regulations indicate that the educational advice must be provided by a qualified teacher who would usually be the head teacher of the school which the child has attended at some time during the preceding eighteen months. If for some reason the child has not been attending school, advice must be sought from a teacher who has experience of teaching children with special educational needs or has a knowledge of the sort of educational provision which the child might need. When a head teacher has not personally taught the child in the preceding eighteen months, the advice should be prepared after consultation with a teacher who has taught the child within such a period. In the case of a hearing impaired or visually handicapped child the advice must be provided after consultation by the head teacher, or special needs teacher, together with a teacher who has an additional qualification for teaching in these specialist areas.

Teachers initially found it difficult to adjust to the more open requests for educational advice after the relatively prescriptive SE1 (which asked for information about the child's performance from the educational point of view). Many LEAs found it helpful to issue general guidelines to head teachers advising them how to formulate their advice. The quality of educational advice improved when guidelines were issued; indeed such guidelines might have been issued earlier, if LEAs had received the various Circulars and Regulations more than two months or so in advance of the 1 April 1983 implementation date.

A copy of the educational advice may be sent by the LEA to the medical officer who will have responsibility for formulating the medical advice.

Medical advice

Medical advice must be sought by the LEA from a fully registered medical practitioner who has either been designated specifically for this purpose or nominated in a particular case by the District Health Authority. In practice the designated officer will normally be the specialist in community medicine responsible for child health who has coordinated the various aspects of medical information from all the doctors who have a relevant contribution to make about the child's special educational needs. Apart from the clinical medical officers, otherwise known less formally as school doctors, examples of more specialist medical officers would include a paediatrician, psychiatrist, neurologist, audiologist, ophthalmologist or orthopaedic surgeon.

The designated medical officer would also provide the advice from the specialist support services such as speech therapists and physiotherapists.

The summary of medical advice is submitted to the LEA in writing by the designated medical officer.

Doctors more than other professionals involved in the assessment had the greatest reservations about the format of their advice; patients do not normally have access to their doctor's records, but the 1981 Act expressly provides that the medical advice on their child be included for ultimate submission to parents. There had to be a new understanding of the concept of confidentiality and an acceptance that circulation of the advice to parents as well as to the LEA was not a breach of medical ethics. Doctors have now adjusted to this new approach and to the fact that their advice can only be of use to other professionals involved with the child and to the parents if it is written in non-medical language. Equally care has to be taken that any comments do not render the medical officer liable to litigation or possible libel. While caution prevails, most doctors welcome the opportunity to write a more open style of report.

Psychological advice

The third stage involves the educational psychologist who may have access to copies of the educational and medical advice before the psychological advice is prepared. The regulations state clearly that psychological advice must be sought from an educational psychologist employed as such by the LEA or from a person engaged as an educational psychologist for a particular case. Any advice from a clinical or other psychologist must be channelled through an educational psychologist.

Other advice

The LEA must also seek advice from others who have a relevant contribution to make to the assessment process. The professionals most likely to be encompassed by this general requirement are staff in the nursing and school services, both of which will have appointed a designated or nominated officer specifically for this purpose. They will have received a copy of the notification sent initially to the parents and will, therefore, be aware of the decision to assess the child's special educational needs. At the same time as the notification is sent the designated nursing officer and the social services officer will be asked if they have any information about the child; in many instances the nursing officer will have no relevant information on the child and should say so in writing; obviously the nursing services will have records on every child in their area, but the information may not be pertinent to the assessment. Such information as is available regarding a child with some form of physical disability or disorder is clearly of paramount importance in relation to the child's needs. Social Services may not have information on such a child, although may have extremely valuable information on children and their families with acute social needs.

Either service may choose whether to take advantage of the opportunity to provide information about the child or advice about how the child's special educational needs can be met.

It has already been stated that separate requests will have been made by the LEA for educational medical, psychological and other advice, including nursing and social services. Other support agencies, for example the education welfare service, local branches of national organizations like the Autistic Society may also have submitted advice, either voluntarily or in response to a specific request from the LEA. The whole essence of Section 5 assessment is based on a cooperative multi-disciplinary approach; many of those who have submitted advice will belong to multi-professional teams. The individual members of the team will provide their own separate professional advice, but the team may also wish to submit its collective view when this seems apposite. This is to be encouraged, particularly when the corporate identity of district handicap teams, community mental handicap teams, child, adolescent and family psychological and psychiatric services, and child development or assessment centres have instilled confidence in the community because of their well established traditions and expertise.

The completion of the assessment

The next stage in the process has been reached when all the information and advice has been collated and the LEA must decide whether the special educational needs should be determined by the preparation of a draft statement. In the majority of cases, the completion of the formal assessment will lead on to the statementing procedure. In a comparatively small number of cases the best interests of the child will not be served by the preparation of the statement. In these cases the LEA must notify the parents of the decision not to issue a draft statement and of their right of appeal against such a decision (Section 5(6) and (7)). (The next chapter refers in more detail to the whole appeals procedure under the 1981 Act). The appeal at this stage must be made by the parent to the Secretary of State for Education and Science, who may direct the LEA to reconsider its decision (Section 5(8)). In practice the appeal would be referred through the chief officer to the officer who signed the notice; this officer may then need to confer with all those who offered advice or information following which there may be agreement to determine the special educational provision by issuing a draft statement. If there were failure to agree, there could be two courses of action open; either the Secretary of State could be provided with a written justification of the reasons for not determining special educational provision for the child, or reference could be made to the authority's appeals committee for an impartial view. It should, however, be noted that this latter course of action has no legal basis in the 1981 Act, although it may help the LEA and the parents to review their respective positions and reverse or confirm the initial decision. As the Act stands the final decision on this matter clearly lies with the Secretary of State.

Examinations

The earlier part of the chapter outlines the procedure for serving on the child's parents notice of the intention to make an assessment; this may require the child's attendance for an 'examination', most likely to be a medical examination or possibly a session with the educational psychologist, although some psychological testing may need to be done without parents being present. Since the child will normally be at school, a formal examination would be totally inappropriate when the educational advice is being prepared.

If any separate arrangements are necessary, the details which can be found in Schedule 1, Part 1, paragraph 2 (as required by Section 5(3) (b) of the Act) state that parents are entitled to attend their child's examination, if they so wish. The notice informing them of the need for an examination shall contain the following information:

1. the purpose of the examination;
2. the time and place at which the examination will be held;
3. the name of an officer of the authority from whom further information may be obtained;
4. the fact that the parent may submit such information to the authority as he may wish;
5. the parent's right to be present at the examination.

Any parent who fails without reasonable excuse to comply with any of the requirements of such a notice, particularly in relation to the child's attendance at the examination at the date and time and place stated shall be guilty of an offence and if convicted be fined a sum not exceeding £50. It is expected that this part of the legislation will only rarely, if ever, need to be invoked, since the majority of parents will wish to participate fully in any enquiries which could benefit their child's progress or welfare.

Children under two years

The assessment procedures described so far in this chapter relate to children over the age of two years, but the 1981 Act also includes arrangements for the assessment of children under two years of age. If a LEA believes that a child either has or probably has special educational needs, an assessment of these needs may, with the consent of the parents, be carried out, but must be carried out if the parents so request.

The assessment would be made in the form most appropriate to the child's needs, age, ability and aptitude. Much will, therefore, depend on the degree of the child's maturity and overall development. For example, in general terms, it will pose fewer problems to assess a young child's coordination, motor control or auditory and visual discrimination than intellectual development. On completion of the formal assessment the LEA may make and maintain a statement about the child's special educational needs in whatever way seems most appropriate. Special educational provision for a child under two years means educational provision of any kind; such provision could include advice and support through home visits or otherwise by peripatetic teachers of the deaf or the visually handicapped, education members of the community mental handicap team or psychologists. It could also include attendance at mother and toddler groups or opportunity groups. In many cases the LEA will be reliant on effective communication links with the Area or District Health Authority, as spelt out in Section 10 of the Act. When a child reaches the age of two, the statutory provisions of the Act come into force.

The statement

The culmination of the formal assessment is the preparation and issuing to parents of a proposed or draft statement. The preparation of the statement should not be an end in itself, but the legal documentation of the child's needs and how they can be met. One would hope that good practice would in any case have produced the same results, but the document may provide some LEAs with the legal justification for providing additional resources at a time of constraint or introduce a degree of coercion on those LEAs which have previously been unable to accord a sufficiently high level of priority to the whole area of special needs.

Section 7 of the Act outlines the full process of statementing. Section 7(1) states that once the decision has been taken to specify the form of educational provision which the child requires at the end of the formal assessment, the LEA must prepare a statement and comply with the terms of the statement. At this stage a detailed set of procedures must be followed by the LEA. Unless the parents themselves make arrangements for the special educational provision identified in the statement, the duty lies with the LEA to make the necessary arrangements (Section 7(2)).

The form of the statement

The form and contents of the statement are prescribed in the Education (Special Educational Needs) Regulations 1983. The format for a model statement was issued with DES Circular 1/83, but the actual design can be decided at local authority level. Some LEAs have designed their own version of the statement, although many have adopted the suggested model which is reproduced in Appendix 3.3.

The statement is in five sections. Part I is an Introduction which includes relevant details about the child who is the subject of the statement, including the child's parent or guardian.

Part II, Special Educational Needs, summarizes the needs identified by all the professionals who submitted their advice with due account being taken of the parents' views.

Part III, Special Educational Provision, specifies the form of educational provision which should be made for the child. Reference must be made to any facilities, equipment, staffing arrangements, curriculum and other arrangements which must be made to meet the child's special educational needs.

Part IV, Appropriate School or other Arrangements, should contain a description of the type of school which the child should attend or the provision to be made if the child is to be educated otherwise than at school, for example at home, in hospital or at a specialist centre. If the name of the school is known it should be stated, unless the parents will be meeting the costs themselves. If the LEA is prepared to meet the costs at one of its own schools, or a school maintained by another LEA, a non maintained or independent school, it should be identified in this section. In the case of children in care or under supervision close cooperation with the Social Services Department is essential to reach decisions about the child's future education.

Part V, Additional Non-educational Provision, must contain details of any provision which will be made by the health authority, Social Services or some other body to support the child's education, if the LEA believes that advantage should be taken of such provision. If no additional arrangements are to be made, this should be stated clearly in this section.

There are various models for arriving at the decision which determines the form of educational provision which best meets the child's special needs. The first model entrusts the formulation of the wording in Part IV to a senior officer of the authority; a variation of this model would enable the senior officer to prepare this part using the recommendations of those who have submitted advice with particular emphasis on the views of the educational psychologist.

The second model reflects more of a teamwork approach; several LEAs have established a placement panel or statementing team, usually of staff employed in the education service. The team would include the education officer, the adviser for special needs and the educational psychologist. In this model the role of the adviser is crucial for it is he who by his experience should be best qualified to interpret which form of the curriculum is correct for the child. Mainstream with support will usually be applicable to the small number of children who can remain in ordinary schools while being protected by a statement. A modified curriculum will be required for the greater part of those children who will be the subject of a statement and who have moderate learning difficulties, or behavioural or emotional difficulties. Those children with severe learning difficulties will benefit most from a developmental curriculum. These three curriculum models, although apparently distinct, form a continuum of educational provision on which the adviser can offer specific advice relevant to the assessed needs of the child. It could, for example, be right to specify principally one of the curriculum models with elements from another; this relatively new approach should ensure that an individual programme can be drawn up in school for each child for whom the LEA maintains a statement.

The proposed statement is dated and signed by a senior officer of the authority; since it is a legal document the name appearing at the bottom of the statement should be the person who actually signed it. As soon as it is ready, the proposed statement should be sent to the parents with an explanation of their rights as to what may happen next.

If the parents disagree with any part of the proposed statement, they may, within a period of fifteen days starting on the day it was received by them, make representations to the authority about its contents and ask for a meeting to discuss it with an officer of the LEA.

If the parents still disagree with any part of the assessment after the meeting has taken place, they have a further fifteen days in which to ask for a meeting with the person or persons whose advice they do not accept and the LEA must comply with this request. In those cases where more than one meeting was arranged, either with the same or several persons the parents have fifteen days in which to make their views known to the authority, starting on the date fixed for the last of the meetings. The intention behind these fifteen day periods is to allow parents time to consider their position about their child's future, the LEA the time to make the necessary arrangements and to ensure that the whole process must be completed within reasonable time limits for the benefit of all involved, particularly the parents.

The officer of the authority whom the parents see at the initial meeting requested would normally be the one who collated all the information and advice and may possibly be the one who signed the statement. If this officer is unable to satisfy the parents, the further meeting or meetings could be with the head or other teacher, doctor, educational psychologist, nursing officer or social services officer or some other individual whose advice was incorporated in the proposed statement or included in any of the appendices or who would be most suited, qualified or experienced to provide explanations or allay anxieties and fears.

It will be of great assistance to the majority of parents if the proposed statement is accompanied by a simple form on which they can indicate that they accept the draft; or would welcome more information; or that they do not accept the draft, stating their reasons. The return of such a form determines for the LEA the next sequence of events.

After taking into account any representations which the parents may have made about the draft statement, the LEA may in accordance with Section 7(8):

1. issue the statement to the parents in the form originally proposed;

2. make a statement in a modified form;

3. decide not to make a statement.

The LEA must inform the parents in writing about which of the options it decides to follow. Once the decision has been taken to make a statement, the LEA must send the parents a copy of the substantive final version of the statement, which in the majority of cases will be identical to the draft when the whole process has been handled sensitively and with professional competence and efficiency. At this time parents must be informed in writing of their right to appeal against the special educational provision specified for their child in Section IV of the statement, and of the name of the person to whom they can apply for information and advice about their child's special educational needs. The Act is not specific as to who this person might be, but could include the headteacher of the child's school, an appropriate officer of the LEA or possibly a voluntary body.

Implementation

As soon as all the legal procedures have been completed, every effort should be made to arrange for the child's admission to the school or unit mentioned in the statement.

An essential part of the preparation for a child's admission is a visit by the parents together with the child to the school named in the proposed statement. Parents can make their own way to a local school, although some will appreciate the offer of being accompanied by an officer of the authority who could be the educational psychologist or the education welfare officer who is already involved with the child and his family. It is perhaps even more important that parents should visit a residential school which could become the child's home during term time, apart from half-term holidays and weekend leave.

The child and parents should not only see the premises and physical aspects of the school, but also meet the teaching and non-teaching staff, especially those who will have direct responsibility for the child's educational development and general welfare. It would be unreasonable to expect parents to accept the proposed statement without first having satisfied themselves that what was being offered met with their general approval.

In some cases the child may remain in the school at which he or she is already registered; this would apply to that small proportion of the eighteen per cent or so of children with special educational needs who attend ordinary schools and who require the protection of a statement to ensure that their needs are fully monitored. In a small number of cases it may be necessary to arrange a provisional or temporary placement until a permanent placement can be secured, eg when a particular school is full and it is known that a vacancy will occur in the near future.

Assessment placements

There is another aspect to temporary placements for which there is no legal basis, although the terms of the Act do not preclude such practices. (See paragraph 16 of Circular 1/83). It has already become apparent that it can take as long as six months to complete the formal assessment, and indeed sometimes even longer. In order to meet the needs of the child without delay and without disregarding the statutory procedures an arrangement which has become known as 'assessment placement' is becoming an established practice in many LEAs. It works like this; if there is some evidence that a child has, or may have, special educational needs, the notice and notification referred to earlier would be sent to the parents. If they accept the decision to make an assessment of the child's needs, they may if it is in the best interests of the child agree, without ultimate commitment, that the child be given an assessment placement, usually while the formal procedures are being carried out. This ensures that a child is receiving special educational provision at a time of critical development. More often than not the proposed and the substantive version of the statement will confirm that the child's placement will become permanent. For the duration of the assessment the child's name should remain on the register of the school from which he was transferred, with an appropriate footnote, and a special register should be maintained at the school to which he has been admitted on assessment placement. If the statement does not confirm the temporary placement, he should return to his first school; if the placement is confirmed, because the school can meet the child's needs, his name should be removed from the first school's register and placed in the permanent register of the other. This procedure is principally intended for provision within the local authority sector.

Confidentiality of statement

The contents of the statement, including all the appendices, remain confidential and cannot by the regulations be disclosed to any parties without the parents' consent, with the following exceptions:

1. to a person or persons who in the opinion of the LEA would benefit from such knowledge in the educational interests of the child;

2. for the purposes of an appeal under Section 8 of the Act (see next chapter);

3. for relevant research purposes on the understanding that in any publication the anonymity of the child and parents is preserved;

4. for the purposes of any criminal proceedings or on the order of any court;

5. to facilitate any investigation which the Ombudsman may be entitled to make in relation to maladministration.

The Regulations also require that, so far as is reasonably practicable, arrangements shall be made to ensure that unauthorized persons do not have access to the statements or their associated documents.

Transitional provisions

Schedule 2 of the Act entitled 'Transitional Provisions' referred to the procedures which should be followed when the relevant Commencement Order came into effect. All those children for whom a LEA was already providing special educational treatment at the time the major provisions of the 1981 Act came into force on 1 April 1983 were deemed to be the subject of statements, even though they had not gone through the new Section 5 assessment procedures. However, it was necessary for LEAs to have issued a statement on these children by 1 April 1984. These became known as 'transitional statements' in local parlance and parents had to be given assurances that this was merely a requirement under new legislation, although nothing may have changed in relation to their child's education. Most LEAs sent carefully worded letters to parents to allay any fears and many headteachers of special schools arranged meetings of parents to explain the new procedures and allow opportunities for questions and discussion.

The transitional provisions referred to two other broad categories of children. The first concerned those who had been through the SE procedures within the twelve month period prior to 1 April 1983 but for whom the LEA had not arranged special educational treatment under the 1944 Act. Such children were taken to have special educational needs and LEAs had to make special educational provision, although were under no obligation to issue a statement until 1 April 1984. Where a statement was issued, LEAs were not required to give details of the assessment of those needs, until a formal assessment had been carried out under Section 5 of the 1981 Act.

The second related to those children who within a twelve month period immediately preceding 1 April 1983 had been examined by a medical officer of the authority to determine whether they were suffering from any disability of mind or body, and if so the nature and extent of such disability, but about whom no decisions had been taken over any requirements for special educational treatment. For a six month period commencing 1 April 1983 LEAs were not required to follow the new assessment procedures under Section 5 of the 1981 Act. If any decisions about special educational treatment were made during the six month period, LEAs were obliged to follow them through as if a formal assessment had been completed, although there was no requirement to issue a statement until 1 April 1984. As with the first category, where a statement was issued there was no obligation to give details of any assessment until a full Section 5 assessment had been completed. It was, however, necessary to inform parents of their right to ask for a full assessment, if they so wished.

This facility for parents to request an assessment was not just restricted to the transitional provision of the Act. Section 9(1) gives any parent the right to ask for an assessment of their child's educational needs, if he is not already the subject of a statement under Section 7; the LEA responsible for the child must comply with such a request, unless in the authority's opinion it is unreasonable. It would be incumbent upon LEAs to provide parents with an adequate explanation, if it were decided not to initiate the normal assessment procedures.

Requests for assessment

If on the other hand, a parent whose child is already the subject of a statement, asks the authority to arrange for an assessment of his educational needs under Section 5 and such an assessment has not been made within the period of six months ending with the date on which the request was made, the LEA must comply with the request, unless it is satisfied that assessment would be inappropriate. These conditions, set out in Section 9(2), could be invoked by parents when there is a possibility that the child's needs may have changed, but there is also protection for the LEA not to proceed if those involved with the child believe that no purpose would be served by a full assessment at that stage.

Mandatory reassessment

Regulations 9 of 1983 (Special Educational Needs) does, however, make provision for the mandatory reassessment of all children who are already the subject of a statement and whose needs have not been assessed since before they reached the age of twelve years and six months. During the period of twelve months beginning with the day on which they attain the age of thirteen years and six months, the authority must reassess the child's special educational needs. It would, of course, be necessary to provide parents with an explanation of the procedures to be followed during the reassessment, for which there are sound reasons; it will enable the LEA to focus on the arrangements which should be made for the remainder of the child's school career, to prepare for the transition to adult life, or to make any necessary arrangements in anticipation of leaving school, including further education, vocational training or employment. The results of the reassessment might even suggest the return of a child to an ordinary school, particularly if some of the child's problems have been resolved or home circumstances have changed. It should in any case be part of good practice in schools to be sensitive to the changing needs or circumstances of pupils, without the formality of statutory reassessment procedures.

LEAs are required to review statements at least annually in accordance with paragraph 5 of Part II of Schedule 1 of the Act. The first review would, therefore, take place within twelve months of the issuing of the statement and thereafter at twelve monthly intervals. The purpose of the review is to monitor the arrangements made for children who are the subject of statements. Circular 1/83 indicates that although the duty lies with the LEA the review should normally be based on reports prepared by the school which the child is attending including reports from teachers and other support staff who are directly involved with the child. Parents should be given a written invitation to submit their views on their child's progress either orally or in writing, and any views should be taken into account in compiling the review.

The term 'formal assessment' has already been used on several occasions in this chapter and relates specifically to Section 5 procedures. The review should be part of the continuous process of the assessment of the child's needs, progress and general development, and not merely a means to an end.

Reviews and reassessments may require either the amendment or withdrawal of a statement or the issuing to parents of a new draft statement. If the LEA proposed to amend or cease to maintain a statement, parents must be given notice in writing of the proposal and be informed of their right to make representations within fifteen days beginning on the day the notice was served. Parents must be informed in writing of any decisions taken about any representations which they make. They could, for example, object to any proposals to alter the content of the substantive statement or, on the contrary, not to altar the statement, if in their view there had been significant changes in the child's needs which would warrant a review of the special educational provision originally proposed and agreed. It is expected that reassessments, either mandatory or carried out on parents' requests would normally result in the preparation of a new draft statement; parents would have the same rights as those to which they are entitled in relation to initial formal assessments.

If a child who is already the subject of a statement moves to another authority, the LEA which made the statement may transfer the statement, but is required to forward the statement if the new authority so requests.

The new authority is under an obligation to identify the child's needs and having done so must serve notice on the child's parents of the proposal to assess those needs, as if it were an initial formal assessment. If the transferred statement was made in the three year period immediately preceding the date on which the notice was served, the new Authority may, with the written consent of the parents, ask the previous LEA for the educational, medical or psychological advice, which formed part of the statement, if it is decided to proceed with an assessment of the child's needs. The former LEA may advise the new LEA that the relevant advice in the appendices to the statement is still pertinent if it is considered that the child's needs have not changed. Any relevant information amassed at the time of the annual reviews should also be sent to the new LEA.

The new LEA must then assess the child's needs in the light of all the advice and information, and representations or evidence submitted by the parents.

The new LEA has three principal options once in receipt of a transferred statement:

1. to issue a statement relevant to the new local conditions, the child's needs and the provision to be made to meet those needs;

2. not to make an assessment, since it is believed the child does not have special educational needs, and inform the parents in writing of such a decision;

3. to follow the full Section 5 assessment procedures, if this seems to be in the best interests of the child and possibly also the LEA.

In these circumstances the parents have the same rights as any other parents under Section 5 in relation to assessment and Section 7 in relation to the statementing procedures. The provisions of Section 9 which refer to requests for assessment can obviously be invoked by parents if necessary, particularly if the LEA has decided not to make an assessment of the child's needs.

It is interesting to note that some of the terms of Regulation 12 of 1983 would not be so vital if there were a greater equality of provision of services generally for children with special educational needs throughout England and Wales.

On a few rare occasions it may be necessary for a LEA to initiate school attendance order proceedings under Section 15 of the Act; this would only happen if the parents failed to ensure their child's attendance at the school named in Part IV of the substantive version of the statement following the completion of the statutory assessment procedures. Once notice has been given of the intention to serve an attendance order on the child's parents, they have fifteen days in which to respond; if the parent selects a school suitable in all respects for the child, including his special educational needs, the school will be named in the order, unless the Secretary of State directs otherwise.

If the school named by the parents is considered unsuitable, the LEA may apply, after giving notice to the parents of its intentions, to the Secretary of State for a direction to determine which school is to be named in the order. It will be necessary to amend the statement if the school to which the Secretary of State directs that the child should be admitted is different from that identified in Part IV of the statement. One hopes that, although ultimately the LEA may have recourse to school attendance order procedures, they can be obviated by judicial use of the Section 8 arrangements for parents to appeal against the special educational provision specified in the statement. Section 16 of the Act explains how school attendance orders can be amended or revoked and the possible consequential effect on the wording in the statement.

A brief reference must be made to other powers which the Secretary of State is given under Section 18 of the Act. If and when any questions concerning the assessment and statementing procedures are referred to the Secretary of State, he may serve notice on the parents requiring them to present the child for examination by a person appointed by him, if he thought advice from that person would help to resolve the question. Although Part I of Schedule 1 is not explicit on the matter, it is not unlikely that a notice from the Secretary of State would contain similar information, suitably amended, to the notice which a local authority would issue under similar provisions when an examination was considered necessary.

It should, however, be noted that the powers of the Secretary of State in relation to examinations under Section 18 can extend to any questions put to him about other aspects of the Act in addition to those concerning assessments and statements.

Each of the stages in the complex labyrinth of the formal statutory assessment procedures has featured in the text of this chapter, and the next chapter concentrates on the appeals procedure. Appendix 3.4 represents a detailed flow chart of the whole process and displays logically and graphically the various steps which are required or may be required, depending on the decisions taken at the previous stage.

Aims of Assessment

The aims of assessment and the professional means by which those aims might be achieved should be reconsidered. The 1981 Act demands that a process be completed, but defines neither the instruments to be used, nor the dangers inherent in a process of assessment.

It should be remembered that the principal aims of assessment are threefold: for classification and diagnosis, for the definition of treatment and for prediction of future capacity and behaviour.

Classification can be regarded as the administrative device to identify broad areas of need, eg moderate or severe learning difficulties. The process focuses attention on broad types of behaviour and curriculum range. Diagnosis follows on to do one of two things: firstly to identify a particular condition, and secondly to isolate specific difficulties and curriculum stages.

When a child has been assessed as having particular needs, a course of treatment must be identified. The direction of curriculum change in special needs education is towards greater clarity of stated objectives for teaching. Assessment is a necessary prerequisite for this emphasis of direction.

Educational planners in school who are developing the curriculum or policy innovators in an LEA need to be able to predict the likely profile of populations of children. Assessment must be both valid and reliable in order to achieve this.

Children may be assessed via three main methods: observation by professional staff at school and occasionally at home, observation by parents in a variety of settings and by the use of instruments which may or may not be standardized. An example of a standardized test instrument is the Wechsler Intelligence Scale for Children; Gunzberg's Progress Assessment Chart is an example of a test which will reflect a child's abilities non-competitively. Any of these three assessment techniques may be used to look at a child's potential for the future, or describe the child's present level of functioning.

Assessment invariably looks at five major areas of concern. Tests of cognition determine what is understood or perceived, and are normally seen as highly significant. Educational tests are used to indicate levels of attainment within curriculum areas, eg mathematics and reading, and seek through diagnostic testing the reasons for difficulties and possible means for remedying them. Thirdly, in depth or case study assessments seek an individualized, often social, profile. Personality assessments (eg Bristol Social Adjustment Guide) seek to establish personal characteristics of children as members of a community. Finally, assessments of motor development monitor the often highly significant influences of physical changes in children.

Those responsible for the multi-professional assessments under Section 5 of the Act should be aware of several common dangers.

Firstly, if a child is asked to perform an unfamiliar task, he may not be temperamentally suited to doing so, yet may not lack the potential to perform the task ultimately. Secondly, the form of instruction required by a test may militate against certain cultures or conditions, and may not measure potential. Thirdly, there are difficulties in recording data accurately; how can one be sure that two different researchers are recording the same thing?

It is also important to consider whether forms of assessment are valid (ie they measure what they say they measure) and reliable (that they measure the same thing consistently at the same level).

The health of children and the environmental conditions under which assessments take place are both highly significant factors in the administration of the process, as can be the effects of a repeated usage of a test, making a child familiar with its demands.

Conclusion

It is essential that those responsible for the assessment of children's needs understand the nature and dangers defined above, since the procedures associated with assessment and statements in the 1981 Act are designed to produce results which are more systematic than their non-statutory 1975 predecessors. The most significant factor about Section 5 assessments is that the parents of the child being assessed are much more closely involved at each stage; they now have the right to offer their own views about their child, be informed about the LEA's intentions and the sequence of events, to protest if the LEA goes counter to their wishes and to be consulted about the way their child's needs are described in the proposed statement.

There were genuine concerns that parents would find the new procedures so overwhelmingly bureaucratic that they would be confused and uninterested. These worries are generally without foundation, since all those within the LEA, the Health and Social Services and the voluntary organizations are united in one aim, namely to improve the quality of life of young people with special educational needs.

When the time comes to revise the relevant sections of the Act in the light of the experience of those who have been operating them, it is to be hoped that any amendments or refinements will serve the same purpose of providing the best possible help for those young people and their families often least able to help themselves.

Further Reading

Special Educational Needs. Report of the Committee of Enquiry into the Education of Handicapped Children and Young Persons, Cmnd 7212, HMSO 1978.

The Education Act 1981.

The Education Act 1981, DES Circular 8/81.

The Education Act 1981 (Commencement No. 1), Order 1981, SI No. 1711 (C.48).

The Education Act 1981 (Commencement No. 2), Order 1983, SI No. 7 (C.1).

The Education (Special Educational Needs) Regulations 1983, SI No. 29.

Assessments and Statements of Special Educational Needs, DES Circular 1/ 83 (Health Circular HC (83) 3, Local Authority Circular LAC (83) 2).

Maternal Responses to Autism, Ian Galletley, MA Thesis (unpublished), University of Durham, 1981.

Appendices to chapter 3

Appendix 3.1

Proposals for integration and liaison for pupils with special needs.

The 1981 Education Act has highlighted the obligation of LEAs to provide for children with special needs in appropriate educational settings – what US Federal Law 94/142[1] called 'the least restrictive environment'. The Warnock Report prompted a rethink, not only of the needs of the two per cent of children who historically have been catered for by special schools, but also focussed attention on the special needs of another eighteen per cent of children currently in mainstream schools. The importance of a reconsideration of the needs of this section of the school population was also stressed by the Schools Council in 1979[2] whose survey of the curricular needs of slow learners led them to conclude that 'of every six slow learners in ordinary schools only three are likely to be in schools making a real attempt to meet their special needs, and of these three only one is likely to be in a school which is successfully meeting his needs'.

This paper aims to suggest ways in which the specialized resources at present concentrated in special schools can be redeployed to the greater advantage of children in mainstream schools whilst at the same time enhancing the educational and social opportunities of our full time pupils.

Hegarty and Pocklington[3] suggest that the range of special educational provision can be thought of as 'a continuum from segregated special schooling to full attendance in a normal class, and that different forms of provision, could be seen as different points along that continuum.'

We propose a continuum which is dynamic rather than static, with movement determined by a child's needs at any given time. We have expressed this in diagramatic form to illustrate the differing provision at each stage. The triangle encloses six levels of provision along the continuum with special school involvement increasing in response to the severity of a child's needs. Some of the techniques routinely applied in special schools may be usefully 'exported' to the mainstream eg advice on readability of text books, whilst other resources operate most successfully in a special school setting. However a great many skills and materials can be appropriately and readily applied at all levels.

The stages of assessment referred to broadly correspond to those outlined in the Warnock Report and it is important to note that there is likely to be considerable overlap between stages. The model assumes co-operation between all those concerned with the child – parents, teachers, Child and Family Guidance Service and other agencies, as appropriate, at every level of assessment. Close liaison between all those involved is essential for effective assessment of the child and the best match between needs, resources and placement.

In the first four levels the child is wholly supported within the mainstream school, using the special school as a resource, to greater or lesser degree. If it becomes apparent that this is insufficient to meet fully all the needs of the child it may be necessary to place the child in a special school where he can receive more intensive help, on a part time or short term basis as necessary. At level 4 placement decisions may have to be taken in a more formal way, possibly involving a Section 5 Assessment and statementing procedures. Alternatively, criteria for such placements may be agreed by the mainstream and special school staff in consultation with the appropriate psychologists and officers of the LEA. A list of proposed criteria for Level 4 placement is appended.

We would expect that the support offered to the individual child and his teacher would generate a rapid growth of specialized resources and skills within the mainstream school.

As this progresses the special school would be in a position to concentrate on its extended role as a resource centre, library and clearing house for the dissemination of specialized learning materials whilst maintaining its current level of care for children with special needs on full time or part time placements.

Suggested selection criteria for children who may be considered suitable candidates for part time or contract placements in special schools:

Positive indications

Positive parental view of placement.
Positive response to questionnaire on child's difficulties.
Learning difficulties with possible resulting behaviour problems.

Anxiety and difficulties in coping with large classes leading to withdrawn behaviour.
Academic performance as measured by agreed tests eg SNAP Basic skills checklist, Neale Analysis of Reading Ability, Life and Social Skills checklist.

Negative indications

Children feeling hostile to placement.
Parental hostility to child going to special school.
Parental inability/refusal to accept child's difficulties.
Child with poor self image likely to be re-inforced by attendance at a special school. .
Behaviour difficulties which are not primarily resulting from learning problems, including aggression and violence and difficulties from poor family functioning.

Liaison should be mutually agreed at the time the placement is organized so that all interested parties are kept informed of the child's progress throughout the period he is in the special school.

Procedures for phased re-integration and a probable time scale should be agreed at the same time.

References to Appendix 3.1

1. The Education of Handicapped Children Act 1975 (PL94–142)
2. *Curricular Needs of Slow Learners*, Wilf Brennan, Schools Council Working Paper 63, 1979.
3. *Educating Pupils with Special Needs in the Ordinary School*, Hegarty, Pocklington & Lucas 1981.

A proposed continuum of educational provision for children with special needs in education

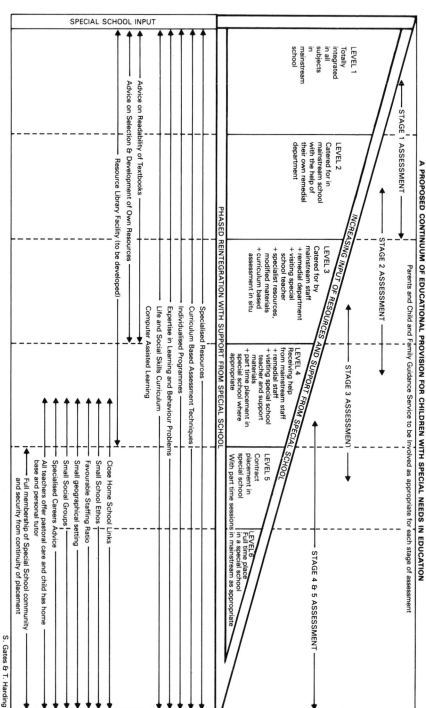

A PROPOSED CONTINUUM OF EDUCATIONAL PROVISION FOR CHILDREN WITH SPECIAL NEEDS IN EDUCATION

Parents and Child and Family Guidance Service to be Involved as appropriate for each stage of assessment

SPECIAL SCHOOL INPUT

LEVEL 1
Totally
integrated
in all
subjects
in
mainstream
school

LEVEL 2
Catered for in
mainstream school
with the help of
their own remedial
department

LEVEL 3
Catered for by
mainstream staff
+ remedial department
+ visiting special
school teacher
+ specialist resources,
modified materials
+ curriculum based
assessment in situ

LEVEL 4
Receiving help
from mainstream staff
+ remedial staff
+ visiting special school
teacher and support
materials
+ part time placement in
special school where
appropriate

LEVEL 5
Contract
placement in
special school
With part time sessions in mainstream as appropriate

LEVEL 6
Full time place
in a special school

STAGE 1 ASSESSMENT

STAGE 2 ASSESSMENT

STAGE 3 ASSESSMENT

STAGE 4 & 5 ASSESSMENT

INCREASING INPUT OF RESOURCES AND SUPPORT FROM SPECIAL SCHOOL

PHASED REINTEGRATION WITH SUPPORT FROM SPECIAL SCHOOL

Advice on Readability of Textbooks
Advice on Selection & Development of Own Resources
Resource Library Facility (to be developed)
Specialised Resources
Curriculum Based Assessment Techniques
Individualised Programmes
Expertise in Learning and Behaviour Problems
Life and Social Skills Curriculum
Computer Assisted Learning

Close Home School Links
Small School Ethos
Favourable Staffing Ratio
Small geographical setting
Small Social Groups
Specialised Careers Advice
All teachers offer pastoral care and child has home
base and personal tutor
Full membership of Special School community
and security from continuity of placement

SPECIAL SCHOOL INPUT

WARNOCK ASSESSMENT STAGES

S. Gates & T. Harding

Appendix 3.2

Des Circular 1/83: Annex 1

(a) *DESCRIPTION OF THE CHILD'S FUNCTIONING*

1. Description of the child's strengths and weaknesses

Physical State and Functioning
(physical health, developmental function, mobility, hearing vision)

Emotional State
(link between stress, emotions and physical state)

Cognitive Functioning

Communication Skills
(verbal comprehension, expressive language, speech)

Perceptual and Motor Skills

Adaptive Skills

Social Skills and Interaction

Approaches and Attitudes to Learning

Educational Attainments

Self-image and Interests

Behaviour

2. Factors in the child's environment which lessen or contribute to his needs

In the Home and Family

At School

Elsewhere

3. Relevant aspects of the child's history

Personal

Medical

Educational

(b) *AIMS OF PROVISION*

1. General areas of development

Physical Development
(eg to develop self-care skills)

Motor Development
(eg to improve coordination of hand and fingers, to achieve
hand-eye coordination)

Cognitive Development
(eg to develop the ability to classify)

Language Development
(eg to improve expressive language skills)

Social Development
(eg to stimulate social contact with peers)

*2. Any specific areas of weaknesses or gaps in skills acquisition which impede
the child's progress*

(eg short-term memory deficits)

3. Suggested methods and approaches

Implications of the Child's Medical Condition
(eg advice on the side-effects of medication for epilepsy)

Teaching and Learning Approaches
(eg teaching methods for the blind, deaf, or teaching through
other specialized methods)

Emotional Climate and Social Regime
(eg type of regime, size of class or school, need for individual
attention)

(c) FACILITIES AND RESCOURCES

1. Special Equipment

(eg physical aids, auditory aids, visual aids)

2. *Specialist Facilities*

(eg for incontinence, for medical examination, treatment and drug administration)

3. *Special Educational Resources*

(eg specialist equipment for teaching children with physical or sensory disabilities, non-teaching aids).

4. *Other Specialist Resources*

(eg Nursing, Social Work, Speech Therapy, Occupational Therapy, Physiotherapy, Psychotherapy, Audiology, Orthoptics)

5. *Physical Environment*

(eg access and facilities for non-ambulant pupils, attention to lighting environment, attention to acoustic environment, attention to thermal environment, health care accommodation)

6. *School Organization and Attendance*

(eg day attendance, weekly boarding, termly boarding, relief hostel accommodation)

7. *Transport*

Appendix 3.3

Statement of Special Educational Needs

I – Introduction

1. In accordance with section 7 of the Education Act 1981 and the Education (Special Educational Needs) Regulations 1983, the following statement is made by the................ council ('the education authority') in respect of the child whose name and other particulars are mentioned below.

Child

Surname........................   Other names ....

Home address ....

....

....   Sex ....

Date of birth ....   Religion ....

Home language ....

Child's parent or guardian

Surname........................   Other names ....

Home address ....   Relationship to child ....

....

....

2. When assessing the child's special educational needs the education authority took into consideration, in accordance with Regulation 8 of the Regulations, the representations, evidence and advice set out in the Appendices to this statement.

II – Special educational needs

(Here, set out in accordance with section 7 of the 1981 Act, the child's special educational needs as assessed by the education authority.)

III – Special educational provision

(Here specify, in accordance with Regulation 10(1)(a), the special educational provision which the education authority consider appropriate to meet the needs specified in Part II.)

IV – Appropriate school or other arrangements

(Here specify, in accordance with Regulation 10(1)(b), the type of school and any particular school which the education authority consider appropriate for the child or the provision for his education otherwise than at a school which they consider appropriate.)

V – Additional non-educational provision

(Here specify, in accordance with Regulation 10(1)(c), any such additional provision as is there mentioned or record that there is no such additional provision.)

(Signature of authenticating officer)

....

(Date)   A duly authorised officer of the
                                      education authority.

....

Appendices to the Statement of Special Education Needs

Appendix A: Parental representations

(Here set out any written representations made by the parent of the child in pursuance of section 5(3)(d) of the Act and a summary which the parent has accepted as accurate of any oral representations so made or record that no such representations were made.)

Appendix B: Parental evidence

(Here set out any written evidence either submitted by the parent of the child in pursuance of section 5(3)(d) of the Act or submitted at his request or record that no such evidence was submitted.)

Appendix C: Educational advice

(Here set out the advice obtained in pursuance of Regulation 4(1)(a).)

Appendix D: Medical advice

(Here set out the advice obtained in pursuance of Regulation 4(1)(b).)

Appendix E: Psychological advice

(Here set out the advice obtained in pursuance of Regulation 4(1)(c).)

Appendix F: Other advice obtained by Education Authority

(Here set out any advice obtained in pursuance of Regulation 4(1)(d) or record that no such advice was sought.)

Appendix G: Information furnished by District Health Authority or Social Services Authority

(Here set out any such information as is mentioned in Regulation 8(d) or record that no such information was furnished.)

Note

The above list follows the wording of the Education (Special Educational Needs) Regulations 1983. The educational, medical and psychological advice will be reproduced in Appendices C, D and E respectively. Appendices, A, B, F and G will consist of copies of the relevant documents, or where none have been submitted, of a note to that effect.

Appendix 3.4

Education Act 1981: Procedure for assessment of children with special educational needs

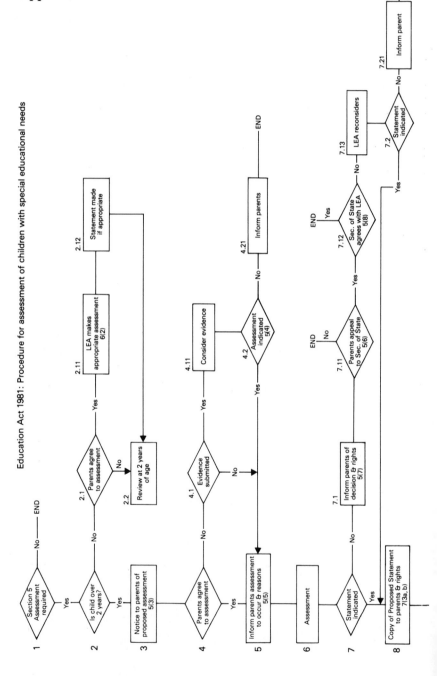

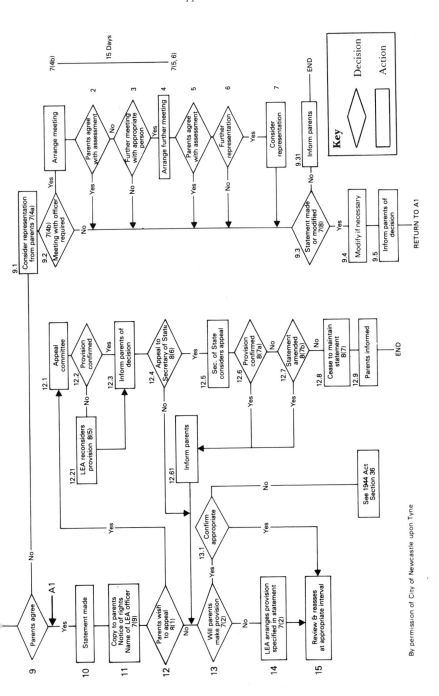

By permission of City of Newcastle upon Tyne

4 Appeals procedures

The 1981 Education Act emphasizes throughout the right of parents to know what is being considered for their children, to have access to accurate and informed information, to be able to put forward their own views and preferences, and to appeal against the decisions of the authority. The rights of access to information and to be able to put forward their own views are enshrined in section 7, paragraphs (4) to (7) of the Act. Briefly, parents must be given the name of an officer whom they can question on any aspect of the procedure, they must see all the professional advice sought by the LEA and they can question those who have given the advice. They can also put forward their own representations, in Appendix A of the statement, and bring forward their own independent professional or other evidence, in Appendix B. These procedures are designed to give parents the maximum opportunity to clarify and question the authority's position, to state their own, and to negotiate a compromise where there is initial disagreement, before they fall back on the formal appeals procedure, with its inevitable confrontation and hardening of positions.

Prior to the implementation of the Act, parents often expressed their frustration in feeling that they could not make any progress towards special educational provision unless the child's headteacher felt it was necessary. If the headteacher said that the child had no special needs parents felt that they had nowhere to turn for a second opinion. Under the 1981 Act the right of parents to an assessment is almost total. An authority may only refuse to assess a child if the child has been assessed within the past six months, or where the request is in the authority's opinion unreasonable. However, the wording of the Act leaves some doubt as to whether this assessment must in all cases be a formal assessment under section 7 of the Act. If the child has previously been the subject of a statement, and falls under section 9 paragraph (2), there is no doubt that the authority must make a formal assessment under section 7 if requested, subject to the provisos of reasonableness and recent prior assessment. If the child has not been the subject of a statement, the authority is bound to make an assessment, unless it would be unreasonable to do so, but the word 'formal', whether by accident or design, has been omitted. It may, therefore, be open to the authority to make an informal assessment only.

If the authority makes a formal assessment under section 5 of the Act, it may after making the assessment decide that it does not consider that the child's special educational needs require the protection of a statement, or in the words of the Act, that it is 'not required to determine the special education provision that should be made for him'. In this circumstance, parents may appeal in writing direct to the Secretary of State, but have no recourse to an Appeal Committee. The Secretary of State may require the authority to reconsider its position, but cannot, under this section of the Act, require it to come to a different conclusion.

Where the authority considers, as the result of a formal assessment, that it should maintain a statement on a child it must, before making the statement, serve on the parent of the child a copy of the proposed statement and written explanation of the parent's rights to any or all of the following:

1. to make representations (or further representations) to the authority about the content of the proposed statement;

2. to require the authority to arrange a meeting between the parents and an officer of the authority at which the proposed statement can be discussed;

3. to require the authority to arrange meetings between the parents and the person who gave the advice in question to the authority.

In due course the authority, having exhausted the machinery for compromise and negotiation, and having failed to get the agreement of the parent to the proposed statement, may proceed to make a statement in the form originally proposed, or in a modified form or not to make a statement at all, and must notify the parent in writing of this decision. In all cases where a statement is made the authority must serve on the parent a copy of the statement, notice in writing of his right under section 8(1) of the Act to appeal against the special educational provisions specified in the statement and notice in writing of the name of the person to whom he may apply for information and advice about the child's special educational needs. Authorities should fix a reasonable length of time – not specified by the Act but not less than fourteen days – during which notice of an appeal must be made. At this stage parents may accept the statement or they may request consideration of the case by an Appeal Committee under section 8 of the Act.

Appeal Committees

The 1981 Act lays down that Appeal Committees shall be constituted in the same way as Appeal Committees under the 1980 Education Act, although they exercise a somewhat different function. It will be remembered that Appeal Committees under the 1980 Act are concerned primarily to decide questions of entry to one particular school for which the parent has expressed a preference, but which the Authority has refused. Under the 1981 Act Appeal Committees can consider any aspect of the disagreement between authority and the parent over the educational provision to be made for a child. Unlike Appeal Committees under the 1980 Act, however, Appeal Committees under the 1981 Act, if they disagree with the authority's provision, can only remit the case to the authority for reconsideration in the light of the Committee's observations. The authority must reconsider its decision, but is not bound to change it. Where an Appeal Committee confirms the decision of a LEA or the authority informs the parent of its decision in a case remitted to it by an Appeal Committee, the parent may appeal in writing to the Secretary of State.

Composition of Appeal Committees

The 1980 Education Act lays down that authorities must establish a panel of persons from whom an Appeal Committee can be constituted. Panel members should comprise members of the authority or of any Education Committee of the Authority and persons who are not members of the authority or of any Education Committee of the authority, but are acquainted with the educational conditions in the area of the authority or are parents of registered pupils at a school; they should not include any person employed by the authority otherwise than as a teacher.

The Appeal Committee should consist of three, five or seven

members nominated by the authority, with members or Education Committee members not outnumbering others by more than one, and not acting as chairman of the Appeal Committee. Likewise, it is advisable that a member of an Education Subcommittee dealing with admission policies should not be chairman of an Appeal Committee. Persons who have taken part in earlier stages of a case should not be members of an Appeal Committee for that case, nor teachers at a school involved in the case, nor persons married or closely related to an excluded member; husbands and wives should not serve on the same committee.

Statutorily, the regulations governing membership of 1980 Act and 1981 Act Appeal Committees are identical, but the DES has expressed the view that an Appeal Committee under the 1981 Act should contain at least one person with some knowledge of special education. In practice, this may not be particularly easy to achieve with the existing 1980 Act panel, depending on how close a knowledge of special education is deemed appropriate. If membership of a committee which includes special education in its remit is adequate, the existing panel may serve; if being governor of a special school, or a teacher in a special school, or having direct personal knowledge of a handicapped child is required it may be necessary to empanel new members to deal with 1981 Act appeals. As with 1980 Act appeals, the chairman should have previous experience in the conduct of hearings.

Size of Appeal Committees

The Act requires that Appeal Committees consist of three, five or seven persons, but experience with 1980 Act appeals shows that too large a number can be daunting to parents. In practice, one of the limiting considerations for the smallest size of committee is the possibility that a committee member may have to leave during the appeal; if there are fewer than three members left the appeal must be reheard by a fresh Appeal Committee; if three or five members remain, and authority members do not outnumber other members by more than one, the appeal may continue, if everyone agrees.

Clerk of the Committee

Each Appeal Committee should have the services of a Clerk, who will remain with the committee when it withdraws (or asks the interested parties to withdraw) to consider its decision. He will assist by offering advice on procedure or law, or by referring to notes of evidence and recording decisions and reasons, but must be seen as an independent source of advice and his role should be explained as such to parents. Although he will normally be an officer of the authority, he should not in the course of his employment deal with the matters under consideration.

Procedure for the Appeal

An appeal must be made in writing setting out the grounds on which it is made and authorities will need to offer parents some guidance on how best to do this; it may be that a *proforma* will prove the most convenient way of providing such guidance, if parents indicate that they wish to appeal. In practice, it will usually be clear from the earlier discussions on the draft statement whether the parents are going to appeal; the statement will either be sent to parents in the knowledge that they have agreed the draft statement, or because consultation over the statement has reached an impasse and the completion of a statement, without parental agreement, and an appeal against it is seen as the only possible way forward.

The proceedings at the hearing of the appeal should be as close as possible to those adopted for appeals under the 1980 Act; while these are not laid down by statute, other than that the Appeal Committee must afford the appellant an opportunity of appearing and making oral representations, the conduct of the proceedings should allow for informality coupled with fairness. Appeals under the 1981 Act will tend to rely heavily on expert evidence, both for the parents and on behalf of the authority, and parents should be invited to provide the Clerk with copies of written evidence in good time before the hearing, so that it can be circulated to members in advance. The written evidence for the authority will similarly be circulated, to members of the Appeal Committee and to parents. Documents relating to Appeal Committees may be sent by first class post to the parents, or delivered by hand. Section 11 of The Education (Special Educational Needs) Regulations 1983 makes it clear that the statement and evidence relating to it, while normally confidential to the authority and the parents, will be made available to the Appeal Committee in the event of an appeal, but care must be taken to maintain confidentiality within these limits.

One method of proceeding at the hearing is set out below, but this may be varied as the committee thinks fit, so long as both parties have the opportunity to put their case.

1. The case for the authority is presented.

2. There is opportunity for the parents to question the authority's case.

3. The case for the parent is presented.

4. There is opportunity for the authority to question the parent's case.

5. Reply and summing up by the authority.

6. Reply and summing up by the parent.

Neither party should be alone in the presence of the Appeal Committee in the absence of the other; both parties will withdraw while the committee considers its decision; should the committee require further evidence or clarification from one party, both parties should attend and both should return to hear the committee's decision which should be confirmed in writing to the appellant by the Clerk, together with the grounds on which it is made. It is important that the decision and the reasons for it are fully and clearly expressed and capable of being understood by a lay person.

Appeals should be heard in private, but a member of the LEA may attend as an observer at any hearing of an appeal in that authority, as may a member of the Council On Tribunals. The Appeal Committee may allow the appellant to be accompanied by a friend or to be represented, and should normally do so unless there are good reasons to the contrary, which should be explained to the parent. However, it is hoped that legal representation will seldom be necessary or appropriate.

Where the Appeal Committee cannot come to an unanimous decision, the appeal should be decided by a simple majority of votes, with the chairman having a casting vote where the voting is equal. It is, of course, always desirable that decisions should be unanimous. No formal record of the Appeal Committee hearing is required, but the Clerk of the committee should keep brief notes of the proceedings, the attendance, the voting and the decisions.

Appeals to the Secretary of State

As has been stated earlier, decisions of the Appeal Committee are not binding on the authority and parents who are dissatisfied with the decision of the committee, or by the decision by the authority if the case has been remitted to it for consideration, have a further right of appeal to the Secretary of State. No formal procedure is envisaged for appeals to the Secretary of State and parents, in being advised of their right of appeal, should be given some guidance as to how to set about it. It is at this stage of the 1981 Act procedures, and at this stage only, that the authority can be directed as to what action it must take. The Secretary of State may, after consulting the LEA concerned,

1. confirm the special educational provision specified in the statement;

2. amend the statement so far as it specified the special educational provision and make such other consequential amendments to the statement as he considers appropriate; or

3. direct the LEA to cease to maintain the statement.

Appeal to the courts

As in any legislative provision a further right of appeal exists through the Courts as to the interpretation of law in any particular case, and so the legality of action taken in that case. Since the implementation of the 1981 Education Act on 1 April 1983, there has been no recourse to the Courts comparable to the appeal in the High Court on 10 May 1984 – the Queen v South Glamorgan Appeal Committee ex parte Dafydd Hywell Evans – on the procedural provisions of Schedule 2 of the 1980 Act. There, it will be remembered, judgement was given that the committee had misdirected themselves, that their decisions should be quashed, and that the matter should be remitted for hearing before a differently constituted committee. The issues being considered in that case – the grounds on which the Appeal Committee could determine that there would be prejudice to the provision of efficient education if the appellant's child were admitted to the school of his choice, and their failure to weigh the degree of that prejudice against the factor of parental choice – are crucial to the conduct of appeals under the 1980 Act and have led to widespread reconsideration by authorities of their procedures and their guidance to Appeal Committees. The case, while it has implications for appeals under the 1981 Act, is not central to them in the same way. In the South Glamorgan case the child to be admitted to a class, which in the authority's submission was already full to capacity, was in no way different from other children in the class. In any case under the 1981 Act, should parents press their claim to education in an ordinary school under section 2 of the Act, evidence on the child's special educational needs and the special educational provision required to meet those needs would be crucial. However, the need to balance the wishes of the parents against the degree of prejudice to the child's own education, to the provision of efficient education for children with whom he would be educated and to the efficient use of resources would be equally relevant in an appeal under the 1981 Act.

It was no doubt the Government's intention in drafting the 1981 Act, as it is the expressed wish of the DES, that authorities should endeavour to accommodate the wishes of parents wherever possible and that the appeals procedure would be used as little as possible. The statutory procedure for the preparation of a statement builds in a lengthy process of consultation with the parent and it is only when total impasse has been reached that recourse to an Appeal Committee becomes inevitable. It is yet too early to judge whether the comparative scarcity of appeals under the 1981 Act is a vindication of this hope, or whether a new generation of parents will have more frequent recourse to an Appeal Committee in the future.

References

1. Education Act 1981
2. DES Circular 1/83
3. Education Act 1980, Education Appeal Committees Code of Practice (ACC 221/81)
4. Education Act 1980, Education Appeal Committee Revised Code of Practice (ACC 05/85) with Annexe 2 – Appeals relating to Special Education.
5. The Queen v South Glamorgan Appeal Committee ex parte Dafydd Hywell Evans case reference number CO/197/84 (Abridged in Education, 8 June 1984 pp 471–2).

5 Integration

'Integration is not simply a new form of provision, another option as
it were. It is a process whereby the education offered by ordinary
schools becomes more differentiated and geared to meeting a wider
range of pupil needs.'[1]
The development of special provision for children labelled as
'handicapped' has had a relatively short and chequered history.
Anyone reading chapter 2 of the Warnock Report will be struck by
the recurrent notion that whilst special provision has been deemed
necessary for many children, particularly those suffering from severe
handicaps, one of the main tenets of legislation from the early part of
this century until the most recent framework proposed by the 1981
Education Act is that where possible children will be educated in the
ordinary school. John Gabbay and Charles Webster maintain that –
'the Warnock Report (1978), and its related White Paper (1980) and
Act (1981) constitute little more than ritual reiterations of a call for
the integration of the handicapped into normal schooling – calls of a
kind which have characterized a succession of official pro-
nouncements since 1954. Ironically, in the meantime the ESN
population in special schools has increased from about 58,000 in
1950 to about 150,000 currently. Waiting lists have been created
because ascertainment for special education has throughout tended
to outstrip the available resources. By the efforts of teachers and
psychologists, the child population in the ESN(M) and ESN(S)
categories has increased steadily since 1950.'[2]
This view of special education, which at first sight appears
somewhat cynical, points to the reality that whilst lip service has in
the past been given to the desirability of integration for children with
special educational needs, only slow progress in attaining this goal
has been made. It can be shown that the developments in special
education during the 1960s and 1970s were concerned to provide
sufficient buildings and classroom resources to accommodate the

identifiable ESN(M) population and to cater sufficiently well for the ESN(S) population which in 1971 was transferred to the charge of education from health authorities. During the 1970s local authorities were much exercised in ensuring appropriate but separate provision for these groups of youngsters since it was quite clear that the ESN(M) population had been traditionally under-provided for. Interestingly during this period of time authorities were beginning to make progress in providing specialized 'on-site' units which were to cater for partially hearing children. Equally during that period an increasing emphasis was placed on the improvement to the curriculum in special schools. Examples can be found throughout the country of schools and local authorities which were, even during this time, concerned to make realistic links between special and mainstream schools. In Oxfordshire, for example, a number of special schools were creating links which involved pupils attending neighbouring mainstream schools for a high percentage of their time. Moves such as this were beneficial particularly in terms of the width of curriculum and access to that curriculum by special school pupils which was unavailable to them in the smaller special school. Similarly, the education of hearing impaired children in units attached to mainstream schools was seen to offer better access to curriculum and therefore improved opportunities for such youngsters.

1981 Education Act

It has to be acknowledged that the advent of the 1981 Education Act which built on many of the concepts identified and articulated in the Warnock Report marked a significant watershed in the education of children with special educational needs. By identifying the problem posed by the labelling of children as handicapped and replacing this by the terminology of special educational need, defined in terms of learning difficulty, the legislation has made a significant leap forward and has undoubtedly enabled people to perceive special education in a different light. Whilst it might be claimed that this move is merely an exchange of one label for another, it is far more significant than merely the change of labels. There is little doubt that the change of emphasis has influenced the way people have addressed themselves to the problems caused by a child's handicap to learning in the normal school environment.

The provisions of Section 2 of the Act, which have been described as a 'charter for integration' and which sent shivers up the spines of many people engaged in special schools at the time of publication, are a clear message to those responsible for making provision for children with special educational needs that such provision should wherever possible be made within the ordinary school. The further requirement of this Section on the ordinary school itself is an interesting and fundamental change in the school's approach to coping with children with special needs. The need to identify children within the total school population who are experiencing learning difficulties has helped to widen the perceptions of responsibilities and to develop awareness of the size and the complexities of the problems which need to be tackled.

The eighteen per cent

Whilst secondary schools have often sought to cope with their 're-medial' children by appointing a small number of remedial teachers or, as in the primary school, to have remedial groups, there has been scant recognition that the problem should be seen in a different light from that of merely remedial teaching. Schools are now increasingly aware of the notional 20 per cent of children who will at some point during their school lives experience learning difficulties. Whilst, in the past, those children who have 'severe and complex needs' ie two per cent of the school population, would have been identified and moved to segregated provision, the notion of the wider population experiencing learning difficulties has undoubtedly changed views about how the whole problem should be tackled. One of the effects of this increased awareness is the increased expectation of schools for resource help. Whilst the 1981 Act makes it quite clear that schools should cope within their normal resources for the eighteen per cent or so of children it identifies as having learning difficulties, teachers who are hard pressed for resources will argue that it is unrealistic to expect them to be able to adopt significantly different curriculum and organizational models in order to cope with these children without additional help. It can be argued that this group of children has been presenting similar problems to the schools for many years and that schools should, by making adequate curriculum and resources provision, be capable of responding to their needs. Whilst this may be true, it does not help schools in responding more positively to their needs. This group of youngsters has been integrated within the school for many years, although it might again be claimed that those deemed to be in need of significant remedial help have often led a segregated life within the school. This is clearly not the case in most primary schools where they would form part of a normal class with, very often, a very wide spread of ability. Teachers in primary schools have, for many years, been concerned at the amount of time they have needed to give to this group of youngsters, very often feeling guilty at the apparent disproportion of time devoted to them. Within the secondary school this group of youngsters may well have received significant and segregated remedial provision during their first two years and then increasingly less specialist help during subsequent years. This type of strategy adopted by secondary schools has worried many teachers involved in remedial education. It has become increasingly clear for instance that the needs of this group of youngsters could be met within mainstream departments providing those departments changed their approach to the curriculum, its content and delivery. For all this, however, we can say that the substantial percentage of children deemed to have special educational needs has always been within mainstream education and that little has changed for them. The fact that this is so normally stems from the difficulties in attracting sufficient resources to what is ultimately a low status group within the school population. At a time when schools are being inveigled into producing better examination results, a wider range of technical and vocational options, increased work experience opportunities, new examination courses and fundamental changes within those courses, it is little wonder that many headteachers will conclude that they cannot afford to direct more resources to their least able pupils. The dilemma of course is that the poorer the curriculum offerings are for the less able the more likely it is that those pupils will adopt anti-school and anti-social attitudes and increasingly present greater problems. The integration of such youngsters into mainstream schools must, it seems, depend upon better resourcing and staffing for schools to meet their needs. Unfortunately the 1981 Education Act with its 'no resource' label has done little to make serious improvements for this group of 'integrated' youngsters possible.

Pupils with severe and complex needs

There is a tendency in dealing with the integration of children with special educational needs in the ordinary school to ignore the largest group of pupils with special needs and concentrate on the integration of those youngsters with more severe and complex needs, ie the two per cent. It is important to acknowledge the work which has always been done by schools in catering for children with special educational needs as defined by the 1981 Act in spite of the fact that resourcing has been woefully inadequate. Having acknowledged this as an important strand in integration, it is appropriate to turn our attention to the integration of the two per cent. It should be noted in doing this that although we have now dispensed with categories of handicap and speak of children with special educational needs in terms of the learning difficulties they have, there are nevertheless different approaches and different values placed on these youngsters. For instance, the school which makes serious attempts to provide facilities for the physically handicapped, the hearing impaired or indeed the partially sighted, may well consider that it is gaining 'bonus points' within the community. The school is seen to adopt a caring role, but its enthusiasm to be seen as providing for the needs of these youngsters may stem from the prestige that it will attract. It is also recognized that many children in these categories are often highly intelligent, articulate and well motivated towards learning and to overcoming the obstacles caused by their handicaps. The same kudos does not always attach itself to those youngsters who have intellectual handicaps and therefore schools may well present contrasting attitudes when looking towards the possibility of integrating different groups.

It will be useful to examine integration and its practice in schools by focussing on the three forms of integration identified in the Warnock Report, namely, locational, social and functional. Locational integration refers to the setting up of special units or classes in ordinary schools but where there is little contact with other children, particularly in the curriculum of the school. Social integration is where special classes or units are set up and where there are opportunities for social interchange, particularly at break times and perhaps even at assembly times. The fullest form is functional integration where there is direct contact with children in the normal school programme and where there is a shared curriculum.

Locational, social and functional integration

It is too easy to comment disparagingly about locational integration. It may be claimed that integration of this kind is not integration at all but merely a superficial response to the whole notion. This is to disparage the very necessary stage which many local authorities went through in determining precisely how integration policies could be developed. An excellent example of locational integration which has developed through the social integration stage and has now reached functional integration are those initiatives which, in the 1970s, saw the siting of units for hearing impaired children on the campus of the mainstream schools. The importance of this evolutionary process in arriving at a stage of functional integration should not be underestimated. It can be recognized with the advantage of hindsight that whilst we would not now be satisfied with locational integration but would go immediately for functional integration, it was necessary to go through the earlier processes. The lack of experience of mainstream schools faced with children with very specific difficulties would have proved too much for the schools in the early stages. Only by the introduction of enthusiastic and committed specialist staff who were initially happy to deal with a wide range of needs was it possible to demonstrate to mainstream schools the possibilities inherent in integration. Increasingly integration was practised in an outward direction from the class or unit into mainstream facilities. This was achieved by persuasion, commitment, enthusiasm and, in some cases, by cajoling. Critical to this venture was the commitment, if not the expertise, of individual headteachers. Although, in the early days, few headteachers of mainstream schools had any experience or expertise in the education of partially hearing children, those who were enthusiastic to develop the service in this way proved to be a great asset. Through their efforts it was possible to introduce the hearing impaired to a much fuller range of curriculum opportunities presented by the range available in mainstream classes. Difficulties experienced by teachers in those classes should not be underestimated. It is a salutory lesson to observe the lack of training opportunities that were available to mainstream teachers faced with a small number of hearing impaired children in their classes. It is to their eternal credit that they responded to a new challenge, often in the face of grave difficulties posed by large class numbers. Some authorities were able to make a slight enhancement of staffing in mainstream schools to oil the wheels of the integration process, but this at best often only allowed the double counting of children for staffing purposes. The benefits to the partially hearing and indeed to other members of the school population were seen to be substantial in that, perhaps for the first time, youngsters came into contact with children who had to overcome substantial obstacles in gaining access to the ordinary learning situation.

It became increasingly obvious to those who were involved in developing the opportunities for such children that the approach to integration through the siting of a class or unit was an obstacle to the true aims of integration. It seemed that the struggle to integrate was largely a battle to gain access to mainstream classes. Often the siting of specially erected units militated against the successful acceptance of handicapped children. The fact that units were often dis-associated from the main building lent force to the notion of separateness. A number of authorities then looked afresh at the problem. Whereas initially units had been built as separate and distinct facilities, often across the playground from the main building, it was realized that while an additional building was necessary because of additional numbers and the need for specialized and specialist equipment, this could be provided in the main building itself, providing that the additional accommodation was then used for some other purpose, ie a general teaching space. Thus it was found that hearing impaired children were being housed within the main school building, either through the use of the strategy previously mentioned or indeed, during an era of falling rolls, in classrooms which were otherwise redundant spaces.

The opportunities for social and indeed functional integration were thus enhanced. However, we are still left with the idea of an appendage or addition to the main school. It is increasingly obvious that the whole concept should be turned on its head. If schools are to accept children with severe and complex learning difficulties as part of their expected complement of children, then the idea of accepting such children on to the normal school and class roll is fundamental. The accepted mode should be that such children are the responsibility of the school, with the local authority providing the specialist teaching and resource backup needed to sustain such youngsters in schools. The norm should be to expect such children to participate fully in the life of the school but to be withdrawn for specialist help as and when the need is identified. This still implies the need for specialist teaching facilities and specialist teachers to be on hand. The emphasis however is quite different from that previously accepted in that integration is assumed to be the norm and withdrawal for specialist help is seen as a necessary addition to the teaching provided by the school.

In considering the possibilities for functional integration within the ordinary school, we need to consider the integration of groups of youngsters with special needs ranging from those with mild intellectual handicaps to those with very severe intellectual and physical handicaps. This process of integration would assume that a child's natural catchment area school should, on the whole, cope with a substantial range of handicaps. Again, this would be unreasonable to expect if one has to consider the substantial investment that has to be made in order to sustain these children. The major difficulty that can be identified given the current mixture of segregated provision which most authorities still have stems from the duplication of resources. For instance, if a small village primary school wishes to take on to its roll a child suffering from Downs Syndrome it may be recognized that the special school which serves that area would conceivably have sufficient space and resourcing to cater for that child without any additional expense, whereas if the child is to be sustained in the local village school, then additional resourcing will be needed. This cannot be sustained on a piecemeal basis without considering the implications for the segregated provision. It would seem sensible to assume that there would be a redeployment, perhaps gradual, of staff from the special school into mainstream schools in order to resource such initiatives. The problem facing authorities at present is getting from where they are in terms of current provision to where they want to be, ie providing a much more comprehensive range of support in the ordinary school. Like most transitional exercises it can be seen that the immediate short-term costs are likely to be substantial in order to change the emphasis of provision and to carry this out within the existing limits of budgets. This represents a daunting task for any authority, faced as authorities currently are with tightly constrained budgets. Whilst special education generally enjoys a good deal of good will from members, officers and teachers, nevertheless there are limitations on what can be achieved within existing resources. Indeed, many authorities are finding that one of the dire consequences of the 1981 Education Act has been an increase in the identification and referral of children needing additional resourses. Whilst the authors of the Act could legitimately claim that the Act in itself did not predicate additional resources or indeed assume additional identification, the reality is that expectation has been raised, identification has flourished and demand has increased enormously. In coping with the dramatic growth in numbers of children with social/emotional behavioural difficulties, authorities have where possible sought to create sufficient resources within their own purview and to draw back on their use of very expensive out-county placements at independent and non-maintained schools. In the event the outcome may well have been that their recently provided in-county provision has rapidly filled up, and the demand having grown still leaves authorities sending virtually the same number of children as before into out-county placements. The overall effect of this has been to increase the budgetary demands. This is a particularly difficult area since the cost of placement of any one child is considerable but often stems from the need to remove a child from its home environment and thereby produces a demand for costly boarding education. Whilst authorities have striven to produce the resources necessary to cater for this group of youngsters, this precludes the use of such resources for other developments within special education. That is not to say, of course, that authorities have not managed to create new initiatives, and many have risen to this challenge. It also means that the proportion of money spent on special education has risen considerably over the past two years.

A radical view

Philosophically there would appear to be no obstacle preventing locational integration of virtually any child who has special educational needs even extending to those children who have the most severe and complex needs. The ideal of educating the full range of youngsters on a school campus appears to be attainable. The fact that many local authorities took responsibility for the most severe mental and physical handicapped children during the changeover in 1971 of the Junior Training Centres from health authorities meant, of course, that these groups of youngsters were housed in buildings largely divorced from mainstream schools. The fact that many authorities again have, since that time, built new schools for this group and have located them very often away from mainstream campuses thereby perpetuating the notion of segregation has not helped. Given the necessary resources to relocate these facilities it can be seen that the addition of buildings catering for these youngsters and sharing some resources such as halls, sports halls and playing fields would bring about locational integration. It might also, because of the close proximity of the two facilities, allow some social integration and contact of the non-handicapped group with the more obvious handicaps presented by children in the severe category. This would be expensive in terms of capital expenditure but not necessarily prohibitively so since many of the existing school resources would be realisable assets for a local education authority. What would be critical is the amount of land available on the campus of mainstream schools and, of course, it would also imply that whilst some schools would take on responsibility for these resources the majority would not because of the sheer logistics of numbers.

Like many initiatives which begin to gain acceptance we would almost invariably say that if we were starting on such developments we would not start from the point we are currently at and the process of integrating children with severe and complex special needs into the ordinary school system is a prime example. Were we to be starting from a *tabula rasa*, then the need to cater for the full range of children in an educational system could be considered with the mainstream school as the starting point. This would allow the concept of the community school to be fully enacted. Provision could be made for the whole range of special needs to be met within the normal activities of many schools. Questions such as the means of physical access for youngsters who are, for example, confined to wheelchairs, could be taken into account when building new schools so that provision for ramping and indeed questions as to whether or not schools are built on more than one level could be taken into account. Specialist rooms to help the partially sighted, partially hearing, physically handicapped and others could be considered at the planning stage. Many of the difficulties which face us at present often have their roots in the types of buildings we have inherited.

The real question to be answered is whether or not a local authority is serious in its intent to follow the framework laid down in Section 2 of the 1981 Education Act. If it is, then it should be looking towards the range of provision that it can provide within the mainstream schools. If an authority continues to maintain its segregated provision for a whole range of youngsters with special educational need, ie separate schools for children who were previously categorized as ESN(M) and for youngsters deemed to have social/emotional/behavioural difficulties and it is still content to use the specialized facilities of the non-maintained and voluntary sector in providing for the needs of a minority of its pupils, then it is unlikely that any huge strides will be made in catering extensively for children with severe difficulties in mainstream schools. Clearly, in order to sustain many youngsters within mainstream provision however tenuously, the local authority will need to consider not only a wide range of specialist teaching facilities but also the need for boarding accommodation. It would be misleading to assume that most neighbourhood schools could cater for a wide range of handicap. The incidence, for instance, of Downs Syndrome children means that, whilst a small village primary school may be able to sustain one of these children for a short period of time, it is unlikely that there would be sufficient specialist help to sustain the initiative in the longer term. Consequently, some clustering will be necessary whereby one school within a fairly wide catchment area can cater for these youngsters. In a large county authority it would, in all probability, be necessary for some schools to have boarding facilities. This would be equally true if serious attempts were to be made to cater for the youngsters currently labelled as having social/ emotional/behavioural problems. At the moment many of these youngsters are catered for in independent schools or in special schools with boarding facilities within an authority. This, of course, perpetuates the segregation of such youngsters from mainstream schools. A serious attempt to enable mainstream schools to cater for a full range of special educational need would mean a massive redeployment of resources and a substantial enhancement of buildings and specialist staff.

If integration into mainstream schools is to be a reality for the majority and if such integration is going to be more than mere lip service to locational integration, then much needs to be done. The implications for resourcing have already been highlighted. The need to engage the staff of mainstream schools in intensive and worthwhile in-service work in order to equip them to cope with children with special needs is of paramount importance and as yet has received scant attention even within those authorities with a high commitment to integration. Some efforts have been made nationally to help with this problem but they tend to be very small compared with the total need for specialist in-service training. One of the prerequisites of successfully coping with children with special educational needs in the ordinary school is a very firm foundation in staff expertise which must come initially from intensive in-service work.

Teachers in special schools

Teaching staff in special schools feel threatened by integration into mainstream schools. In those cases where the roll of the special school has fallen as a result of policies to integrate more children into mainstream schools the question of the redeployment of staff from special into mainstream schools has been highlighted. Many staff in such schools feel that their identity as specialist teachers will be lost in the mainstream setting and fear additionally that the needs of the youngsters whom they have in the past dealt with in small teaching groups will also be lost and neglected in the larger school setting. Additionally, many staff are concerned about their career prospects. Within the context of the special school the possibility of promotion to senior post, ie to head or deputy is reasonably clear and possible. In the mainstream school the staff feel that they would be forced into something of a blind alley which would have as its maximum career potential head of department stages. This fear may be somewhat irrational in so far as there is nothing to say that a specialist in special needs should suffer a deterioration in career prospects when compared with, for instance, a specialist mathematician or language teacher. This could, of course, be a transitional problem rather than a long standing one but many staff in special schools do see an erosion of their career status and prospects were integration to impinge significantly on the notion of the special school.

It would on the other hand be unfortunate if new developments in mainstream schools were not seen by teachers from special education as bringing new and exciting possibilities in terms of careers. The expertise that such teachers could bring to mainstream schools would help those schools to meet many problems which they currently encounter with their '18 per cent of children with special needs'. Not only can teachers from special schools bring a clarity of thought in the development of programmes of work but they could also use their expertise to develop and initiate significant in-service training in the school and also in the wider spheres of in-service within an authority. The development of resources in the ordinary school to help a wide range of children with special needs would be a tremendous boon to those schools, and it is in these areas that teachers who were formerly in special schools should develop their future careers.

The value of integration

> Integration is a means, not an end in itself. Pupils with special needs do not need integration. What they need is education.[3]

Integration of children with special needs into the mainstream school should only proceed if it can be shown that the advantages of such a programme out-weigh any disadvantages that might be inherent in a process of integration. Integration in itself is not a

particularly worthy goal unless the opportunities presented to youngsters with special needs are enhanced from that which accrue to them in the special school. There is no doubt that the special school community in so far as it is concerned with a very specific group of youngsters and develops its expertise, its delivery of curriculum, and its organization is geared entirely to meet the needs of a specified group. Many children flourish in such environments. The difficulties come from an acknowledgement that ultimately children are part of a larger world and will have to fit into that larger world as they grow up. Segregation at an early age means loss of contact, loss of knowledge of the 'normal world' and largely a lack of adjustment to that world. Children attending special schools are segregated from their peer groups and form friendship groups often based on handicap rather than normality. It can be claimed then that the social disadvantages which derive from a segregated schooling out-weigh any curriculum advantage or pastoral advantage that may accrue from being part of a specialized community. Integration into mainstream schools can largely overcome these handicaps but only if the issue is treated seriously, and if the needs are adequately recognized and the status of these youngsters is sufficiently high within the ordinary school to merit appropriate treatment. To assume total integration of all children with special needs is probably to make too large a claim. It is likely that there will always be a small number of children who will continue to need very specialized help in small segregated units. Nevertheless the notion that the ordinary school must make strides to offer a wide range of curriculum options for all its pupils is an attractive one. Providing always that the schools can be resourced sufficiently well to allow the opportunities to develop and flourish then it is quite clear from the experience which has been gained so far that the move towards greater integration at a functional level is beneficial not only to children with special educational needs but to other children who come into contact with them. It is to be hoped that the resources necessary to bring about true integration can be made available but that requires large scale commitment not only on the part of the schools, the teachers and the local authority but also by central government.

References

1. *Educating Pupils With Special Needs In The Ordinary School* (page 14), Hegarty & Pocklington, NFER 1981
2. *Oxford Review Of Education* Gabbay & Webster, 1984
3. *Educating Pupils With Special Needs In The Ordinary School* Hegarty & Pocklington, NFER 1981

6 Post-sixteens and the transition from school to work

Provision for the handicapped school leaver has in the past been very much a neglected sector. The numbers of post-sixteen year olds staying on at school or continuing in further education are much lower for the handicapped than for those without handicap; in 1977 only 5.6 per cent of a sample of eighteen year olds ascertained as handicapped were still at school or in further education, compared with 29.2 per cent of the non-handicapped. The neglect may be due to a number of factors – the complexity and variety of handicaps, the fact that at sixteen the statutory period of full-time education ceases, a fatalistic acceptance that little could be done: whatever the causes, the absence of or inadequacies in current provision led the Warnock Committee to identify the provision for young people with special needs as one of their three areas of special priority. In spite of this, subsequent legislation made no mention of the post-sixteens. Even so the last decade has witnessed growing interest and concern on their behalf. There has been a greater awareness too that a range of skills and attainments is potentially within the reach of many with disabilities, and also that those who are most disadvantaged have the most acute needs. Warnock itself generated public interest in and focussed attention on the needs of the handicapped; while the activities of pressure groups, MENCAP in particular, have spotlighted existing deficiencies and have drawn attention to the statutory obligations of local authorities to meet them.

The LEA's statutory duty

The statutory situation as regards the LEAs duty is somewhat ambiguous. The duty under Section 8 of the Education Act 1944 includes the provision of full-time education suitable to the re-quirements of senior pupils, (that is, those under nineteen years of age), other than those catered for under further education. Section 41 of the same Act requires the LEA to secure provision of adequate facilities of further education – that is, full-time and part-time education for persons over compulsory school age. It is uncertain how far those duties extend: whether, for example, they extend without limits to providing a school place with suitable education for every sixteen to eighteen year old, if requested, or similarly if preferred, suitable placement in a college of further education. In practice, LEAs generally follow the Warnock line that there is a duty to provide continued full-time education for all between sixteen and nineteen who want it, either in school or in further education, though not necessarily in whichever the individual prefers. A DES report in 1981 on 'The Legal Basis of Further Education'[1] advocated clarification, but the government has so far taken no action. The uncertainties remain, although the Secretary of State is understood to have indicated his intention to issue guidelines to LEAs on their obligation to provide education for all sixteen to nineteens on demand.

In the meantime the Warnock interpretation of the LEA's duty has moreover been reinforced by the judgement in regard to Oxfordshire and the post-sixteen education of a mentally handicapped pupil. This is understood to have determined the attitude of government departments who tend to adopt the view that LEAs have an obligation to provide post-sixteen education but not necessarily at a particular kind of institution.

What is not in doubt is the entitlement, legal and moral, of the handicapped teenager to a good education. In general terms, the definition of this is the same for all, whatever their abilities or disabilities, and according to Warnock it has two goals: to enlarge a young person's knowledge, experience and imaginative understanding, awareness of moral values and capacity for enjoyment; and secondly, to prepare him for entry into the adult world as an active participant and responsible contributor, with the maximum capacity for independent living. How these goals are translated in educational terms depends on the nature and capacity of each individual; in regard to the handicapped, for example, extra needs arise which require special means to meet them; physical handicap involves creating the maximum facility for mobility, while in the education of the mentally handicapped the acquisition of living skills and learning to cope with the exigencies of everyday life play a significant part. For all who may be able to earn or contribute to their keep, vocational skills will also be important. However varied may be the individual needs, preparation for transfer from school to the world outside is crucial; whether the transfer is from the segregated environment of the special school or from the integrated setting of a mainstream school, problems will have to be faced of adjustment and of meeting the demands of society at large. What then is there on offer?

Provision in schools

The special school   The starting point is of necessity the provision that already exists. For some years there have been mounting pressures, mainly from parents, for children at special schools to stay on after reaching school leaving age. This may be due to an awareness that, particularly with the severely mentally handicapped, they are unprepared or insufficiently mature to leave the protective environment of the school; but it may also be a consequence of lack of suitable alternative provision in further education. Certainly, the trend is markedly so amongst pupils with severe learning difficulties: it is estimated, for example, that the number of sixteen to nineteens staying on in their special schools increased from a third (of that age group) in 1981 to a half in 1983.

This is in line with Warnock's recommendation that pupils who can benefit should be enabled to remain at their special schools after sixteen. LEAs' capacity to meet this is facilitated by falling numbers in other age groups, either as a result of falling rolls or as more have been integrated in ordinary schools. It raises the issue, however, as to what they receive when they do stay on, and whether the teaching resources are such as to provide a meaningful educational experience; or whether it is an uneasy period of marking time to avoid or delay the trauma of entry into the outside world. It should be said that many schools have made strenuous and creditable efforts to cater well for those staying on after sixteen, and at a time when extra resources have been virtually non-existent. There is a good deal of evidence, too, of special schools making real efforts during pupils' two years before leaving age to prepare them for their next stage in life; while the time after sixteen, used as an opportunity of further assessment or of preparation for entry to mainstream courses at school or in further education may be well worth while. Where links exist with colleges, they supply easier transition to further education courses; while the opportunities for assessing students better enable the colleges to fit their provision to the students' needs. It has to be conceded, however, that such an approach has greater relevance for the less severely handicapped. Regrettably the severely and the multiply handicapped are likely to remain those for whom the inadequacies of present provision are most apparent.

The ordinary school   The practice is widespread of accommodating handicapped pupils on an individual basis both in sixth forms and earlier when suitable arrangements can be made, for example for the physically handicapped. Increasingly a wider range of handicaps is being provided for, sometimes on a part-time basis for particular specialist subjects and sometimes full-time with extra support staff in cases, for example, of sensory handicap. Many LEAs in recent years have pursued a policy of siting new special schools as near as possible to existing comprehensive schools to enable handicapped pupils to have the opportunity of some normal school experience. With the requirement of maximum integration following the 1981 Education Act, involving much more effort to provide effectively for handicapped pupils in ordinary schools, with or without attached units, post-sixteen provision for pupils thus integrated becomes simply a matter of normal progression to sixth forms. The broadening of sixth form studies in recent years, moreover, has increased the capacity of schools to cater for varied needs and abilities. Initiatives such as the Certificate of Pre-vocational Education and the Technical and Vocational Education Initiative, which are aimed at making the curriculum more relevant to the needs of pupils for whom A levels are too academically biased, are also intended to cover the needs of some handicapped groups. But again what is available in the sixth form, whether in an eleven to eighteen school or a sixth form college, is likely mainly to be of benefit to the mildly handicapped and those with physical or sensory handicaps for whom suitable premises and equipment can be provided. For the severely handicapped there is little on offer.

Further education

Until fairly recently, special provision in further education for the handicapped student was minimal. Individual students of ability might have special arrangements made for them to enable them to participate in normal courses, but these were exceptionable. For the rest, again a minority, a limited number of places was available at residential institutions, such as Hereward College, Coventry (the only LEA college of its kind), and colleges and centres provided by voluntary organizations such as Rudolf Steiner and the Spastics Society. But for most handicapped there was little else until the recent awakening of interest which has stimulated action in the further education sector.

For handicapped students, and particularly those whose education has been in segregated schools, the further education college has much to offer. It provides a more adult atmosphere, daily contact with students of widely differing skills and outlooks, and an introduction to a less protective environment, with new disciplines, new approaches and attitudes both to learning and to living and maybe eventually to the world of work. The strength of further education has been its flexibility and its capacity to respond to need. But where so much depends on local initiative, the result is a picture of wide diversity and inequalities in different areas. A former Permanent Secretary at the DES, Sir James Hamilton has observed that whereas at the two ends of the spectrum, schools and higher education operate within a relatively well-defined structure, non-advanced further education presents the impression of a variety of courses, institutions and organizations whose diversity borders on confusion. He queried whether its capacity to respond quickly and effectively was sufficient justification for its moving so close to the frontier between diversity and confusion. Recent developments, admittedly piecemeal and uncoordinated, have nevertheless produced a range of facilities for the handicapped, including link courses, introductory courses and full-time college provision.

Courses linking school and college are not new; they have occasionally run adrift both in regard to the selection of students and problems of coordinating and timetabling and ensuring continuity in curriculum. When such problems can be overcome, they are of immense value in introducing the handicapped student to a wider environment. They constitute also a period of assessment and of vocational experience, though for the mentally handicapped the latter is usually subordinate to training in life skills and communication. Link courses are on the increase, especially for those with moderate learning difficulties, though there are many examples of provision for a wider range of handicaps, including severe learning difficulties, hearing impairment and visual handicaps. Link courses may also cater for pupils integrated in ordinary secondary schools as well as for those attending special schools and units.

Additionally to link courses, college provision ranges from a limited scale of admissions on an individual basis to normal courses with minimal special arrangements, through bridging and transitional courses aiming at eventual mainstream admissions, to special provision for a variety of handicaps. Of these there are many examples, one of the most noteworthy being supplied by the North Nottinghamshire College of Further Education[2], with its Work Orientation Unit, set up in 1970. Work preparation, vocational education and training are provided for most handicaps, including the mentally handicapped, deaf, blind and physically handicapped, with opportunities also for abler students to take courses leading to recognized qualifications. A significant example of pioneering effort is the project at Bridgend College of Technology, which in its planning stages anticipated and subsequently fulfilled Warnock recommendations. The scheme comprises a residential hostel for physically handicapped students, adaptations to college workshops and other college premises, and a specially designed course, which operates at three stages to suit differing needs and levels of achievement, and embraces basic and preparatory experience as well as providing opportunities for those able to enter the normal college courses.

But notwithstanding the achievements of a number of LEAs, the picture is an uneven one. Even LEAs with a relatively full and varied provision, moreover, have still to rely for some specialist residential places on out-county colleges and centres maintained by voluntary agencies, such as for example the Queen Elizabeth's Training College, Leatherhead, which provides vocational training for disabled young people.

In providing for the handicapped in colleges, the practical aspects of access and of adaptations to buildings are important. Here the lead has been taken by central government. Circulars issued by the Architects and Buildings Branch of the DES have supplied advice on such matters as improving access and the requisite standards of lighting and of workshop and laboratory provision for handicapped students.

In further education arrangements for the handicapped, there has been a tendency to emphasize the importance of vocational skills. This has been entirely justifiable in helping to equip them for work through which they can become self-supporting, or at least may contribute towards their upkeep and acquire a sense of independence. It is also a factor which helps towards self-respect. The so-called work ethic may be outdated but it is still a fact of life that self-respect comes from an awareness that a person has something to contribute on which society places a value, something one can offer which is recognized by payment. Notwithstanding developments in society which may necessitate some re-thinking of this attitude, the development of skills and an awareness of the world of work is likely still to be an important element in what further education can offer to the handicapped.

But the acquisition of technical skills is not the whole story in regard to doing and holding a job. Other factors are important – personality, social skills, the capacity to communicate and to get on with people and to conform to and accept the disciplines imposed, such as punctuality, application to the job and regular attendance at the workplace. There is plenty of evidence that many handicapped young people show exceptional commitment to their jobs and their employers, but there is also plenty of evidence that failure at work and the reluctance of employers to engage disabled workers are often due less to lack of technical or professional skills than to social incompetence and behaviour faults, which are themselves much less readily remediable through training than deficiency of skills. Work at the University of Oregon (see page 186) with the severely mentally handicapped has shown that although skills can be taught involving delicate manual operations such as assembling complicated electrical equipment, they are not transferable in such a way as to enhance the capacity to cope with the needs of everyday life. Living skills have to be separately taught. An appreciation of this is demonstrated by the importance given in further education courses to developing self-help skills, life and social skills and training in self-confidence and a capacity to participate in group activities. Arts and crafts, music and drama, have also a role in this process of personality development and socialization. It is thus no narrow concentration on practical skills but, to use an overworn cliché, an education for life that is increasingly the aim.

Careers guidance and counselling

Providing for the continuing educational needs of handicapped students requires good liaison between school and college in regard to course continuity and planning. There is need, too, for support and guidance for the students themselves; this involves collaboration with and between two specialist agencies of the LEA – the school psychological service and the careers service. The former should provide information and records of the students' needs, aptitude and potential, and should help to determine what further education would be appropriate. The advice should continue preferably after sixteen, and should be available to all staff concerned.

The careers service should play a parallel role – first, in the years immediately before sixteen, secondly in advising on suitable courses and placements, and thirdly as an agency for counselling and advice after sixteen, whether in continued education or in some form of training or employment. Straddling both education and employment, it is much more than an agency for placing people in jobs. In collaboration with careers teachers in schools, the careers officers have an educative role, helping young people to make realistic and informed choices about themselves and their futures; at the same time they constitute the links between employers, colleges, training agencies, students and parents.

Their work in regard to the handicapped, for whom the availability of education and employment can be very problematical, is highly specialized, and it has become the practice for LEAs to employ specialist careers officers for work among the handicapped. The Warnock Committee envisaged an extended role for them – to act as 'named persons' providing a single point of contact during transition from school to adult life. No government action has been taken on this recommendation; indeed, it is doubtful whether, with the added pressures of rising youth joblessness, this additional responsibility could be undertaken by careers officers without substantial additional staff resources. Even so, they perform a vital function both in advising on options and in monitoring subsequent progress. This clearly impressed the Warnock Committee who recommended the employment of at least one specialist careers officer for every 50,000 of the school population. The Committee also remarked on weaknesses in the guidance sometimes given and mentioned in particular excessively rigid assumptions as to what tasks people with particular disabilities might or might not be capable of.

There is an inherent danger in making assessments and forecasts of a person's aptitudes and potential to which all staff, psychologists, careers officers and teachers need constantly to heed – the danger of predictions of such rigidity as to operate as a limitation on what a person might with education and training be able to achieve, which may be exacerbated by the tendency to concentrate on disabilities rather than on abilities. However carefully compiled, all assessments should be subjected to scrutiny and reappraisal and where necessary modified in the light of the students' progress. This in turn will depend on the availability in each profession involved of enough suitably trained and qualified staff to deal with the handicapped students' continuing needs. Since the professionals most closely and constantly in touch with the students will be the college teaching staff, their role is an important one in a variety of aspects – in course construction, in assessment and in counselling. How colleges use their staff for these functions varies locally, but in any event a member of staff of some seniority would seem essential to coordinate the work. Directing the variety of skills involved imposes a heavy responsibility; while the task of securing an adequate share of college resources for the handicapped is both difficult and delicate in the face of competing claims from other departments working towards more obvious and recognizable professional and academic goals.

Adult training centres

It is a sad reflection on our further education system that the greater the handicap the fewer are the opportunities. Dean's survey in 1983[3] revealed that fewer than one in ten colleges made any provision for those with severe learning difficulties. The main provision for them on leaving school has been outside the education service altogether; namely, the Adult Training Centres run by local authorities' Social Services departments. Originally set up with the limited aim of providing day care and some kind of occupational activity for the mentally handicapped, mostly living at home, ATCs have worked hard to free themselves of this narrow image. Efforts have been made to develop a more positive role of training not only for living skills but for such employment as may possibly be within reach. Pressures for this have mounted. A more enlightened approach to educability has stimulated social services as well as education: while deteriorating employment prospects have had a dual effect. Firstly, the loss of openings for the unskilled has accentuated the demand for more training, since the higher the level of skills the less restricted is the range of options. Secondly, because there are fewer jobs, those who might otherwise have been in employment are swelling the demand for places at ATCs.

These growing pressures both in regard to quantity and quality of ATCs create an acute problem of resources for a service which is perennially under-funded. There are at present approximately 500 centres with about 41,000 places. This falls well below the DHSS yardstick of 150 places for each 100,000 of the population, which one assumes to be a notional target but which predictably offers no financial strategies for its implementation. Qualitatively too, there are deficiencies. A National Survey 1972–77 revealed inadequacies in the education and training programmes, attributable to such factors as uncertainty of objectives and lack of national guidelines. Instructors felt isolated and, aware of their deficiencies, were anxious to develop and consolidate their professional skills; but opportunities for initial training were unsufficient, with little or no in-service training available either.

To create a more coherent approach, Warnock recommended that 'there should be a specifically educational element in ATCs and day centres and that the education service should be responsible for its provision'. Although the recommendation has not been adopted, it has not prevented the growth of a variety of forms of collaboration between ATCs and education. These often consist of links between ATCs and further education colleges; there are instances also of tutors supplied to ATCs by the adult education branches of the service. Clearly departmental boundaries can be overcome without central direction, though in its absence deficiencies are less likely to be rectified where drive, imagination and good inter-departmental links are lacking. On the positive side, some ATCs are changing their title to indicate their changing role and are becoming known as Social Education Centres. At one such Centre, each student's programme is individually agreed by consultation between the Centre, the student and the family. Some are placed on work experience schemes and others attend link courses in college or adult education, often in ordinary classes. Open classes are also held in the Centre for non-handicapped students living in the area.

Progress too has been made in devising suitable curricula for ATCs, notably that developed under the Habilitation Technology Project at the Hester Adrian Centre, Manchester. Known as the Copewell System, it is a comprehensive curriculum, with teaching aids and materials, and consisting of four sections – Self Help, Social and Academic, Interpersonal and Vocational. It is considered suitable for use with handicapped adolescents not only in ATCs but in special schools and in further education.

In spite of progress being made, some doubts remain. Anxieties are felt, for example, by some parents in whose minds the old image of the ATC still lingers. There are fears, too, that the young at ATCs risk being overwhelmed by the presence of elderly handicapped: Warnock in fact considered it very important that there should be separate arrangements for young people in the centres. The worry too remains that with more demand for places the more severely handicapped may increasingly be excluded.

Adult and community education

Although it has normally little to do with the needs of school leavers and training for jobs, community education in a variety of ways in a number of areas is making a significant if unobtrusive contribution to meeting the needs, social and educational, of handicapped students of widely differing ages. Possibly because of its long experience in catering for vastly differing skills and backgrounds, with the main common factor a desire to learn, the service has responded both in providing special programmes and in integrating some handicapped in ordinary classes.

Remedial and basic education has grown in scope and momentum from its early beginnings as the Adult Literary Scheme of a decade ago and it now functions within the overall direction of the Adult Literacy and Basic Skills Unit. It provides a 'second chance' for those who for a variety of reasons left school with an incomplete grasp of basic subjects, and who, with more maturity and better motivation, wish to remedy their deficiencies. It can also be a focal point for other agencies; for example, as well as running its own basic education classes, including living skills and creative pursuits, one centre has established links with the LEAs adult centres, with ATCs, the hospital service, and with some voluntary organizations for which it supplies tutors.[4] At this particular centre, about 25 per cent of the enrolments in September 1984 were mentally handicapped (some with physical handicaps also), mostly attending special groups.

The Youth Service has also contributed to the facilities available for the handicapped. Gateway and PHAB clubs have been sponsored and take place within ordinary youth centres promoting activities which bring the handicapped and non-handicapped together.

While adult and community education, including the Youth Service, has much more to do with informal education and leisure pursuits than with academic and vocational studies, it can supply a valuable range of activities in which some handicapped may participate. Regrettably it is under-valued by those who see it merely as a frill, and it tends to be amongst the first victims of cut-backs in the kind of economic climate that has prevailed in recent years.

The Manpower Services Commission

New schemes of work preparation, experience and training have been provided through the various initiatives launched by the Manpower Services Commission which was established in 1974 as an agency of the Department of Employment. They have included Youth Opportunities Programmes, work experience on employers' premises, Community Industry, and more recently the Youth Training Scheme. Defined as 'an effective integration of skills, knowledge and experience through planned and supervised work experience and properly designed opportunities for "off the job" training or further education', YTS schemes are run through the collaborative efforts of industry and commerce, local authorities, voluntary organizations and consortia of various kinds operating under the control of Area Manpower Boards. The aim is to provide training and experience for disadvantaged teenagers who are unable to get jobs. Though not geared directly to the needs of the handicapped, they have had particular relevance for all who in the current employment situation find themselves struggling at the bottom end of the job market. The generally favourable reations to proposals to extend YTS indicate that even amongst its critics there is an appreciation of the purpose served by YTS during a critical period for young people unable or unlikely to get work.

Attitudes of LEAs to MSC projects have been varied and dichotomous. While there has been suspicion and even resentment at the encroachment upon fields where education has hitherto been in control, the resources available to MSC cannot readily be rejected, especially when they have funded schemes that LEAs would in any event have wished to carry out but which, without MSC money, would have been impossible. So while the arrival of the wealthy interloper has not been entirely welcome, many LEAs have, albeit reluctantly, taken advantage of MSC resources to provide a variety of schemes, open in many instances to the handicapped and supplying them with training facilities that would otherwise not have been available. An excellent example of what can be done with a vigorous and imaginative approach is supplied by Birmingham, which has included the following in its YTS: a Community Placement Scheme, with placements available for the handicapped, an industrial unit for supervised industrial placements, a Special Needs Unit, with emphasis on improving education and living skills, a workshop/skill training base for the deaf, and an Action Resource Centre, together with college-based schemes offering a range of vocational training courses.

But one major question remains: what happens when the training ends? Does the experience gained serve merely to raise vocational expectations which are impossible of fulfilment and may always remain so? Training for work that does not exist may only postpone entry to the dole queue and may serve to intensify a sense of disillusionment. In practice, job creation and training initiatives of the MSC have provided some alleviation for the problem of youth unemployment, but it remains no more than a palliative. What then is in store for the handicapped in a job market when so many trained non-handicapped teenagers are joining the ranks of the unemployed?

Work opportunities and life without work

For the disabled school leaver the task of finding work has never been an easy one. The ideal is of course to work normally alongside the non-disabled, but even during the era of full employment it tended to be a minority, the mildly disabled, who managed to secure ordinary jobs. The Disabled Persons (Employment) Act 1944 required employers with more than 30 workers to employ three per cent disabled; but with its loopholes it has failed to work in practice and targets have not been achieved. At present with the combined effects of recession and rapid changes in technology and automation, opportunities for the disabled in the open labour market have become increasingly remote.

Sheltered workshops, such as are provided by the government through Remploy and by some local authorities and voluntary bodies, while they constitute segregated employment, are better than no employment at all: though the absence of a training function was noted by Warnock as a deficiency. It is arguable of course that much more could be done to facilitate the employment of handicapped people; for example, by providing better support on the job, by environmental modification in the design of workshops, and by restructuring or reorganizing processes to bring them within their capacity to perform. It has also been argued that technological developments may themselves result in the breaking down of complex processes into tasks capable of being done by the mentally handicapped. A further suggestion is that, as a consequence of high energy costs there will be a move towards more community-based activities with more work opportunities for the handicapped both in production and in support services in the close-knit communities that will result from declining mobility. In any event, while accepting the present reduction of work opportunities as a consequence of technological developments, it has nevertheless to be acknowledged that the scale of opportunities for handicapped and non-handicapped is affected by the level of economic activity and general prosperity. Changes, for example, in world trade or in national economic policies will directly affect future job prospects, including those of the handicapped.

Even so, in the light of recent and current trends, it is realistic to make a reappraisal of objectives in the education and training of the handicapped. Here we face a dilemma, neatly expressed by Jackson[5]: do we continue to emphasize the acquisition of vocational skills in the knowledge that few will obtain jobs? Or do we pursue their vocational goals less vigorously and thereby deny some students the possibility of competing for the rare jobs available? One approach, which is already happening in colleges of further education, is to concentrate more on familiarizing students with the general aspects of the world of work, in preference to training in job-specific skills. But a much more radical approach is needed to prepare people for a life without work.

Though the job situation has worsened rapidly in the meantime, Warnock did address the problems of significant living without work – the lack of a sense of purpose, the loss of variety in environment and in human contacts that going out to work provides. Warnock suggested that handicapped folk might be involved in helping one another and in providing voluntary services to needy elements in the community. Taking part, too, in cultural and recreational activities supplied by community education and the Youth Service will help; but in regard to education and training it seems inevitable that vocational preparation must give way to training people in skills capable of enriching their personal lives and unrelated to jobs. Education for leisure becomes not just the vague aspiration of the theorist; it holds the key to a satisfying life-style for many of those who may never have the chance to do what is traditionally known as a day's work.

The overall scene is a patchwork of positive activities and in-itiatives, punctuated by gaps and deficiencies, particularly in the provision for those with severe learning difficulties. The best of current provision is very good indeed, revealing imagination, com-passion and expertise. But what is being done depends very much on local initiative and may seem uncoordinated, growing out of what already exists rather than as a consequence of deliberate policy or planning. The absence of clear policy guidelines is indeed seen by many as a major obstacle to progress. The flexibility and scope that exists for meeting diverse needs by a diversity of approaches has to be weighed against the disadvantages of uneven standards and perhaps even failure to meet minimum requirements. A consequence of uneven standards is that what is available to the handicapped depends on the accident of residence rather than upon the extent of need and potential. What is urgently needed to rectify this inequality and to bring all to the level of the best is a clear government initiative to produce a national plan for further education and training for post-sixteens based on the Warnock principle of regional self-sufficiency. A determined government effort should also include funding: resources, though not the whole story, are essential both to sustain current levels of provision and to make possible future progress. The creation and maintenance of a high level of public support and understanding is also important, for in the final analysis it is attitudes – those of employers, fellow students and workers, and of the public generally – that will determine how the handicapped person will fare, in education and training, in work remunerative or voluntary, and in society as a whole.

References

1. *The Legal Basis Of Further Education*, HMSO 1981
2. *What Sort Of Life?* P Rowan, NFER 1979
3. *Learning For Independence*, Dean & Hegarty, FEU/NFER 1984
4. *Provision For Young People Over 16 With Special Needs*, EMIE/NFER 1984
5. *Integrated Programme For Handicapped Adolescents & Adults*, R I Brown (Editor), Croom Helm 1984

Further Reading

Beyond The School Gate, J Bookis, RADAR 1984
Stretching The System, Bradley & Hegarty, FEU/NFER 1982
The Warnock Report, HMSO 1978
Skills for Living: A Special Needs Document, FEU 1982
Further Education, Training & Employment Opportunities For Handicapped People, National Bureau for Handicapped Students 1981
The Education Of The Handicapped Adolescent, OECD 1981
16–19: A Future for All, NAHT 1982

7 Health and other support services, and voluntary organizations

It is characteristic of the child who has, or may have, special educational needs that a number of professional people or agencies will be or become involved with him/her and the family. This response is intended to be, and generally is, supportive to them in fully developing potential and in coming to terms with a handicapping condition where this exists. From time to time in some cases, and maybe frequently in a few, the variety of support offered is in itself confusing to an already anxious family. By the same token, schools and individual teachers will receive immensely valuable help from supportive agencies and from parents but may equally on occasions be confused or made anxious in their task as a result of inadequate understanding of the respective roles and boundaries of the supportive agencies. In emphasizing the considerable contribution made by other services and voluntary organizations to the assessment of and provision for special educational needs, this chapter will focus on some of the problems of effective communication between the agencies concerned and most importantly between them and the child's parents.

Although a distinction is made here between health services, mainly provided under the NHS, personal social services provided by local authorities, and voluntary organizations, it is recognized that operationally there is very close collaboration and overlap between them in providing specific services which will vary from area to area. Historically, the medical profession has played a large part – some would say dominant – in the field of special education, in collaboration with and development of the often pioneering role of voluntary organizations; and the importance of personal social services is increasingly being recognized, particularly where there is a link between a child's special educational needs and his family circumstances or where a long-term caring or supportive role is indicated, which has traditionally fallen to the NHS or a voluntary organization to fulfil.

Ever since Hippocrates first uttered his famous oath, the doctor has exercised a powerful influence on and in society. In special education the doctor has played a dominant role which latterly has been put into truer perspective in line with the emphasis in the Education Act 1981 on *educational* needs and provision rather than upon specific handicapping conditions, a shift of emphasis which has considerable philosophical, practical and organizational implications. The provision of services is now rightly based largely upon assessment of individual need and less dependent upon the pioneering approach of individuals within a profession or voluntary organization. Support systems are replacing institutions as services are provided at local level and, in so far as it is practicable, in the child's normal setting or community. In the last 100 years, statutory obligations to provide services have been clearly established and reflected in vastly expanded national and local provision. As statutory provision has increased, voluntary organizations, for so long pioneering creators and maintainers of institutions, have moved towards the supportive, and to some extent 'pressure group' function which they now have. Alongside the development of statutory services has come the growth in the number and scope of professional organizations committed to the promotion and improvement of the professions themselves as well as the services provided by its members. Inevitably, as the systems have grown and become more sophisticated (reflecting the quest for ever finer tuning of assessment techniques and comprehensiveness of provision), so they will in themselves give rise to problems, the resolution of which is rarely possible now, if it ever was, through the decision of one of the professionals involved. The development of the NHS, as seen from the LEA administrator's point of view, demonstrates both the positive and negative aspects of a devolved, locally delivered service: good, open communication between the professionals concerned and, crucially, with the client, is essential.

Support services within the National Health Service

As has already been mentioned, the Health Service and in particular the doctors have played a powerful role in the provision of special education, as in the decision-making aspects of assessment and placement of children or in making provision in hospitals or educational establishments run by doctors. This outmoded model is being replaced by an essentially advisory and cooperative function. A doctor may still have a primary role to play in the diagnosis and treatment of a handicapping condition but has an essentially advisory function in terms of assessing the child's learning difficulties and the effect of the handicap on those difficulties and the educational provision required. This shift of emphasis should not be attributed solely to the requirements of the Education Act 1981, specific and far-reaching though these may be. The Health Service is evolving a different philosophy of service delivery, which is essentially community based although there are considerable difficulties both nationally and locally in resourcing this development adequately.

There have also been significant changes in the structure of the NHS and of the professional disciplines operating within it. It has undergone two reorganizations, in a period of less than ten years, which have inevitably affected special education. The first, and more profound, led to the creation of Area Health Authorities and District Health Authorities, embracing those community health services, including major aspects of the School Health Service, which had formerly been the responsibility of the local authority. Since the School Health Service was and remains operationally the most important part of the Health Service in advising and supporting LEAs, this was a move of great significance to the field of special education. Worthy of particular mention was the creation of specialists in community medicine, especially those in child health. Once established, at a senior level within the Health Service structure, these posts provided a clear reference point both within the health authorities themselves and for local authorities in relation to changes in the School Health Service more generally and in the Health Service approach to special educational needs in particular. As a result of reorganization, health authorities defined more clearly other important roles (eg area or district speech therapist or physiotherapist) which provided clearer coordination of specialized services in the field of special education and a good framework on which LEAs could build in responding to the Education Act 1981.

An awareness of the needs and deficiencies of the health and medical services in the wake of the 1974 reorganization led to the setting up of the Court Committee, whose Report *Fit for the Future* was published in 1976. This stressed the need for a child and family-centred service with professionals adequately trained and experienced in the special needs of children. It advocated one service which would follow the child's development from pre-school years through school and adolescence, and an integrated approach to health care which is especially necessary for handicapped children and their parents. It recommended furthermore that each school should have in first line support a school doctor and nurse; for special schools the school doctor would be a consultant paediatrician. The recommendations appeared at the beginning of a period of acute shortage of resources and few have unfortunately been implemented.

Even so, whatever may have been the shortcomings in the 1970s following the first reorganization – and there must presumably have been some to justify a second reorganization less than ten years later – the creation of AHAs and DHAs set the pattern for the delivery of community health services which still obtains with its greater emphasis upon local and locally accountable systems and decision-making. It is difficult to comment on the effectiveness of this approach within the Health Service itself, but it has to be said that in some larger authorities at least the abolition of the AHA structure has led to a diversity of approach and provision between Districts which has not always been helpful to the LEA in meeting special educational needs.

Nursing services

Whereas the family doctor retains the primary responsibility for the health care of families, the community nurse or health visitor, who is increasingly to be found attached to the family doctor's practice, is vitally important, particularly in the early identification of developmental delay, in advising on or arranging assessment and in seeking to ensure that provision is made. This may take the form of investigation or treatment (eg in a case of suspected hearing loss, or where there is a need for stimulation or compensation which indicates that a place in a family centre or nursery school would be helpful). The community nurse is able to make an early and significant input to the network of paediatric services which act as the focus for the pre-school assessment and surveillance of children with a variety of health and developmental problems. Through regular discussions and meetings, which usually do and certainly should include representatives of the education service, the network of services, in which the community nurse often acts as 'key worker', can assess when and in what form to intervene.

After a child has reached school age, when almost by definition most children with learning difficulties will be properly identified and assessed, the nurse attached to each school will have a vital role to play in surveillance, advice on care and management and, in a linking role with other NHS resources – especially the school doctor – for initial or further investigation of problems.

The development of community based services, of which the community nurse is an excellent example, brings both advantages and potential problems. There can be little doubt that this approach represents the most effective way of providing this service, just as within the school, many aspects of learning difficulty are dealt with as part of the school's general organization and by the 'ordinary' teacher rather than by specialist teachers or by withdrawal from classes. However, a process described by the Warnock Committee – most infelicitously – as 'sensitizing the profession' is required, both within the separate disciplines and between them. The community nurse, in discussing the developmental problems of a pre-school child with his parents, must have a good understanding of the facilities available through the local education service and of the service's likely response to the problem, without in any sense pre-judging the outcome of any further assessment of a specifically educational nature. In the same way, the nurse working within the school must be sensitive to the needs and approach of the head and of individual teachers in establishing her general role and in giving specific advice about individual children. Conversely, teachers should be sensitive to the limitations of the nurse's job brief and in particular not seek advice or action inappropriately. This is a general point and problem which needs to be kept in mind in any multi-disciplinary context, which can all too quickly become inter-disciplinary conflict, particularly where the boundaries between the various disciplines are not clearly understood both at a general inter-authority level and in working relationships more locally. If it seems that the point has been somewhat laboured, it nevertheless must be made forcibly and borne in mind, because the attitude of anxious, defensive parents towards 'services' is frequently formed in the early years of the child's life, before the child enters school. Assessment, both informal and formal, can be made easier or more difficult depending on the success and sensitivity of early intervention on the part of the health services, for whom the community nurse is frequently an early ambassador. Fortunately, the disciplines concerned do generally recognize the need for effective communication, and that this has to be worked at.

The doctor

Clinical medical officers (the title may vary from district to district but this seems to be the most common designation) working in the community health service and mainly specializing in child health continue to have a great influence in the field of special education. Particular attention is drawn to the following:

1. In the case of the pre-school child, the CMO is the liaison point with paediatric and other medical consultants, with other specialized services within the NHS, with local social services staff, and crucially in our context, with the education service.

2. The CMO acts as coordinator of medical assessment and advice to the LEA for pre-school children and those already in school.

3. The CMO acts as adviser and support in schools to children and their families, and to headteachers and class teachers in confirming or eliminating health factors as part of their consideration of a child's known or suspected learning difficulties.

4. As a general contributor to the network of services in an area (eg as a member of the District Handicap Team or provider of inservice training) devoted to special educational need.

Mention has already been made of the changes in the role of the doctor generally, and the school doctor is no exception. The LEA and the individual school turn to the school doctor for the initial assessment of a medical problem (or in order to establish that there is none) and for advice on the implications in the classroom.

Speech therapy

This has perhaps been the most undervalued aspect of community health provision in the past, certainly insofar as it affects special education; it appears to be growing as demand grows for advice and support to teachers in the area of language development, increasingly recognized by schools and educational support services such as educational psychologists as a major factor in developmental delay and learning difficulties. In partnership with the teacher, and preferably working alongside the teacher in the school rather than from a base in a clinic, the speech therapist can have a significant effect on progress and make a far greater contribution to the educational provision than the actual time commitment involved would seem to suggest.

This is another example of a discipline within the NHS which is understandably committed to the development of its own professionalism as well as the service it offers. It is usually the case now that the speech therapy service in a health district is organized through a district speech therapist, through whom advice on specific cases as well as more general liaison with the education service will be effected. It already seems likely, as a result of the Education Act 1981, that the growing demand for the advice and support of speech therapists will bring pressure to bear upon District Health Authorities and upon the NHS generally to train and employ more staff.

A major task facing the Health Service and LEAs, in the light of this pressure and fast-growing demand, is to establish the special role of the speech therapist and to define to what extent there is an overlap with the work of the teacher; and to what extent their roles are exclusive, not only in order to avoid duplication and confusion but, more positively, to make maximum use of scarce resources. Articulation problems, for so long regarded as the most important part of the speech therapist's job, are only really severe in a relatively small number of cases; but even in such cases it is increasingly clear that the speech therapist plays an advisory and support role to a considerable extent, as constant practice is carried out by the parent or the teacher, or under their surveillance.

Physiotherapy

As a final example of the community health services available to, and much used by, the education service in providing for special educational needs, the physiotherapist offers a more specialized service to probably a much smaller group of children numerically. It is no less important for that, as a vital input to the development of children with specific handicaps, degenerative diseases, and those who have suffered in road traffic accidents, as well as providing advice more generally to teachers and parents who worry about clumsiness and posture. Again there is a shift of emphasis towards working in an advisory mode, which brings the same benefits and potential problems identified above in connection with speech therapy; and implies that the same sort of pressure for increased staff will be generated not only as a result of changes in ways of working but also because of competing demands for existing resources from other client groups, notably the elderly. The education service, already inured to coping with the effect of the decline in the child population on the resources available must also appreciate the pressure upon other services concerned with supporting special education to reallocate staffing resources particularly to growth areas.

Other health support services

There is not sufficient space here to detail the many other aspects of Health Service provision which come into play from time to time in assisting the LEA with the assessment of, and support for, children with special educational needs. The audiological service, for instance, will be heavily involved with the numerically small but in other ways highly significant group of children whose degree of hearing impairment may cause or contribute to learning difficulties and for whom some special educational provision is required. Occupational therapists, working either in the NHS or for a local authority Social Services Department, may be called upon to advise the LEA or individual schools about the adaptations required or available for severely disabled children. Psychiatric medicine remains a key service in providing for the assessment and treatment of children with emotional and social difficulties which impinge upon their educational performance. In every instance, it is evident that there is a commitment to collaborative work and a greater emphasis than was the case in the past upon advisory work as part of a network or team. This is very much in line with the approach in the regulations flowing from the Education Act 1981 and accompanying joint circulars from the DES and DHSS, where the importance of joint working is stressed. It is also clear, in relation to many Health Service functions as it is in relation to the education service, that the proper delivery of services to children with special educational needs will involve additional finance and manpower in spite of assumptions to the contrary at the time of the introduction of the new legislation.

The following general comments summarize the themes which have gone before in relation to the role of the health services. Firstly, there is the crucially important matter of service delivery (another infelicitous phrase!). With the increasing emphasis upon *educational* needs, and on meeting those needs wherever possible within the ordinary school; at a time, moreover, when they were engaged in a reorganization, the various community health services have demon-strably come up against dilemmas and confusions as to how to meet not only the demand of LEAs for a different emphasis in the assessment of children but also a commitment to provide the services which they had identified as being necessary in a variety of places and in support of potentially a far greater proportion of the teaching profession. To some extent at least in the past, and increasingly so as services became more specialized, clients/patients had been expected to go to the provider of each specialist service (eg in hospital, out-patients departments and clinics). In the context of providing for *educational* need, and with the stress upon provision in the classroom, both LEAs and health services have been faced with the need to deliver the service *where the pupil is*. One criterion for measuring the effectiveness of the new legislation will be the extent to which the services jointly have recognized, validated and committed themselves to providing for this. At the same time, both services need to be alive to the danger of fragmenting long-established provision in order to res-pond not to new needs but rather to needs which have been identified and assessed in a different way, with different objectives in mind, namely providing support in an educational setting and not treatment in a health care setting.

Secondly, serious ethical considerations can come in to play, either in relation to individual cases or to procedures more generally. This is not the place to debate the various ethical models which are un-doubtedly a powerful factor affecting such matters as confidentiality, the sharing of information; and the establishment of mutual trust and respect between disciplines. There can be very few circumstances where the withholding of important information from a child's teacher is justified, but there are regrettably still many examples to be found of this sort of problem. It has to be recognized that teachers do have day-to-day responsibility for, and actual care of children for a very large proportion of their early life, and both local authorities and health services must continue to work away at eliminating this problem of information sharing. If the concept of 'parents as partners' is to have real meaning, moreover, then the importance of sharing information by and between all professionally concerned with a child must be accepted.

Thirdly, and as an illustration of how the last point might be developed, common training experiences should be planned. The Education Act 1981 in itself provides many opportunities for this, which many authorities, both health and education, have already grasped.

Having once been the major provider of services for children in need of 'special educational treatment,' the health services remain a major source of support and expertise for the education service in making appropriate provision under new educational legislation. For the future there should be a continuing emphasis on the screening/preventive role of the paediatric service, on early support for children and their families where developmental delay is identified or suspected, and on arranging early educational intervention where appropriate; and on providing support to the schools once the child is in school. It is equally important that the school and the individual teacher should be supportive to health service personnel, in assisting with observation and assessment. After all, the teacher does spend more time with the child than anyone else except the parent, and is specifically concerned with all aspects of a child's development.

Local Authority Personal Social Services

Social Services staff of the local authority represent the other major support service for LEAs in meeting special educational needs, although in many respects their position is rather less clear than that of the Health Service, either in terms of their contribution to assessment or of support to schools. For example, the statutory involvement in the assessment and statement process relies upon their being notified of an LEA decision to carry out a formal assessment, and not being specifically required in each case to provide advice.

However, there are many important ways in which social workers and their colleagues support the LEA. First and foremost is their involvement, in cases of special educational need, as the agency in whom parental rights are vested, either fully or partially. Close liaison is necessary between the two departments as a whole and on individual cases with individual social workers who will and should be involved in decisions over assessment and provision, whether that be informal at school or as part of the formal process leading up to a statement. It would be all too easy to assume that because two departments of a local authority are involved – and more often than not of the same authority – there will be no problems in agreeing about the provision to be made. From time to time, and understandably, there will be differences of view: the social worker may have views or beliefs just as strongly held as those of 'natural parents'.

There may be other pressures, too. The LEA may be forming the view that the child's special educational needs can only be met in a residential placement where specialized help can be given. The social worker, following departmental policy, may be looking to arrange substitute parenting – adoption or fostering – where, in the interests of establishing or developing family relationships it is essential that the child should be at home. In these and many other circumstances, there are various shades of conflict and difference of opinion and approach between the two agencies. There has always been a higher proportion of children in care with special educational needs than in the child population as a whole: and it may be that the LEA actually finds such cases more complex in their determination, not less.

The point is worth making yet again that in such circumstances there should be a clear understanding between the two agencies at policy-making and decision-making level and in local contact between, say, headteacher and social worker. This understanding should embrace not only the respective statutory basis for provision and involvement but also an appreciation of the boundaries and limitations of each other's role so that expectations are appropriate, not unrealistic. That in itself would not overcome the problems but should facilitate their resolution.

The second substantial area of overlap between the Social Services function and special education occurs where the latter is a direct provider of services such as day or residential centres for children and their families, the emphasis now being upon day care wherever possible. Such facilities may play an important part in early intervention in cases of developmental delay or emotional/social problems (eg mentally-handicapped children). Family centres provide support for young children and, increasingly, for their parents, for whom they offer relief and guidance at the same time as the child has the opportunity to develop outside the context of his family and their difficulties. Such centres will vary from area to area in their number, availability and according to the prevailing philosophy of care; but all provide other agencies, especially the Health Service, with a focus for observation, assessment and shared provision. The education service, too, has the opportunity to use these facilities for the same purposes, as well as to provide early advice and intervention in preparation for a subsequent educational placement. Given that the Social Services Department has quite specific powers and duties in relation to pre-school provision, and given the emphasis which is rightly placed upon early intervention, it is vitally important that these opportunities for cooperative working are fully exploited. Of course, by no means all of the children in such centres will be found to have special educational needs, certainly not in the formal sense of the term, but it is likely that a high proportion will have at some time in their school life.

Community Homes with Education (CHEs), which grew mainly out of the former approved schools, are now fast disappearing as specific residential provision made by, or funded by, Social Services Departments on a regional basis. They provide (mainly residential) facilities for some of the most difficult young people, those in trouble or at risk in some way. This expensive provision is now thought to be inappropriate for many of the young people for whom it has traditionally been recommended; and indeed there is little positive evidence to suggest that it has been successful in other than a custodial sense. The general move to find alternative solutions has profound implications for the education service, not only in the field of special education – indeed, it is a matter of fact that many of the young people concerned do not have learning difficulties – but more importantly in the fact that they have not in the past remained within the local education system but have been educated separately in the CHE. As such establishments disappear, the education service and individual schools will have to provide for a group of troubled and troublesome youngsters who may without proper support cause problems for school organization out of all proportion to their relatively small number.

Finally, mention should be made of the specific provision made by Social Services Departments for mentally- and physically-handicapped children and young people. Establishments providing for these two groups generally do so after statutory schooling has ceased but some centres or homes do provide, both short term and long term, residential care for children, particularly for children who in educational terms have severe learning difficulties. It is important that there should be the sort of liaison between such establishments and schools as would be evident with a responsible parent, together with an understanding on both sides of the special factors involved (eg practical factors such as transport arrangements, shift work of staff; and the particular problems which may arise in school with a group of children who also live together). Adult Training Centres and Day Centres provide further training and education for the mentally-handicapped and the disabled. Strong links with the schools previously attended – usually a special school – are required, not only as a matter of general understanding of the young person concerned but also to ensure a smooth transition in terms of detailed knowledge of what has gone before as a basis for further development. Increasingly, the education service and personal social services staff are realizing the value of continuing education beyond age nineteen for the mentally-handicapped, although there are considerable resource problems for both services in attempting to meet this need.

There are many other ways in which the roles of the education and personal social services overlap and provide opportunities for a cooperative approach to their clients (eg on Intermediate Treatment Schemes or in the discharge of a Supervision Order for failure to attend school.) Clearly, not every child concerned with, or the responsibility of, the Social Services Department will have special educational needs, but the proportion is likely to be higher than average. In terms of good communication and understanding, LEAs could do more to help schools to understand the legislative framework within which Social Services operate and the emphasis which is thereby given to the individual social worker's role, particularly in relation to disturbed or delinquent children. Equally, those responsible for the personal social services system and those working in it should understand those statutory aspects of the education service which seem to have a crucial, and often frustrating, effect on their work, such as school attendance requirements; the organizational factors inherent in large establishments which may make it difficult to give sufficient attention to individuals; and the fundamental function of the school which is to offer an appropriate education to *all* of its children, which may again lead to a clash with individual interests from time to time.

Voluntary Organizations

In a very real sense the present system of special education sprang from the initiative of pioneering individuals and organizations concerned with the effects of handicapping conditions on children during their early formative years. Chapter 2 of the Warnock Report makes interesting and informative reading, both as a confirmation of this historically and as a description of the subsequent development of the role of voluntary organizations which have sought to fill gaps in the statutory services as the latter evolved. The gaps are much fewer in number now, thanks largely to another aspect of the voluntary organization role, namely that of pressure group and lobbyist.

At local level, branches of well-established organizations campaign for better or more services locally; and new organizations form to promote new causes or more specialized aspects of long-established areas of need. Nationally, the larger organizations such as MEN-CAP exert considerable influence through lobbying in Parliament or nationally mounted campaigns. Such organizations played a significant part in the setting up of the Warnock Committee and in pushing through the Education Act 1981, for instance.

There are many organizations nationally concerned in some way with special educational needs, and many more locally, often taking the form of local branches of national bodies. Their role, whether at national or local level, is now completely different compared with even twenty years ago. Historically, they have been major providers of establishments providing services, including education for both adults and children with clear handicaps eg the early schools for children with sensory handicaps; or institutions for socially deprived or abandoned children amongst whom there were a high proportion with handicaps or retardation – what we would probably now term 'developmental delay'. These establishments were largely dependent in early days on local or individual philanthropic initiative, although a network of national bodies gradually emerged. Without dwelling on the past we should nevertheless recognize, as did the Warnock Committee, the fundamental role played by voluntary bodies in making specific provision and in encouraging local and national statutory services to take this over and develop it to the extent that we see today.

Whilst some voluntary bodies remain providers of establishments and specific services – indeed, regulations have for many years recognized the particular role of the 'non-maintained' school – many are now mainly or entirely dependent upon financial support from local authorities (eg The Royal Schools for the Deaf and schools run by Dr Barnardo's.) It is increasingly the case that such establishments offer highly specialized provision for children with very special needs which local authorities cannot easily and effectively provide for themselves, or may not need to because the provision made by the voluntary sector is good. Such provision is now mainly national and regional in character as LEAs either on their own or in cooperation with others within an area aim to meet their own needs. A number of establishments in the voluntary sector have either closed or radically altered their function as a result, and in this connection mention should be made of the considerable increase in provision made by the voluntary sector for the further education and training of handicapped young people. This is a further and relatively recent illustration of how the voluntary sector has seen a gap in services and moved into it to make much needed provision. Already, however, in this respect local authorities are catching up and attempting to meet this need, not only because of pressure to be doing so but more positively because they feel that in many cases more local provision, and specifically allowing the young person to remain at home in his family and community, will be more effective. The reasons for the change of emphasis in the voluntary sector are many and complex, but it is worth highlighting the following;

1. Legislative changes have defined much more clearly the duties of local authorities and have increasingly given statutory force to initiatives, developments and good practice.

2. Perspectives and philosophies have changed, and continue to develop especially in the emphasis on provision within the local community and in the ordinary school wherever possible, rather than on a residential basis possibly many miles away.

3. Cost-effectiveness is an important factor in these days of financial constraint for public services in general and for the education service in particular. It must generally be true of LEAs that they are looking for ways to redirect the considerable resources devoted to sending children to expensive establishments outside their own system to enhancing their own local service.

In common therefore with the statutory system, we find that voluntary bodies in the present day are mainly providing support, and in a variety of ways. Some of the larger agencies, such as MENCAP with their regional officers and RNIB who provide a peripatetic service for some local authorities, employ their own professional staff, who support clients directly and also organize services either on behalf of their own organization or in collaboration with statutory agencies. Local branches, with or without the support of their own paid officers, can identify local problems and needs, liaise with the local authority and NHS and thus try to ensure a good match between locally perceived needs and local provision. They also form a mutually-supportive group of people, usually parents of children who have and present similar problems. In each of these respects there is the same need for good understanding and communication: between the professional officers of the voluntary bodies and the local authority and NHS staff (and for that matter between them and DES and DHSS nationally); between the members of the voluntary organizations and local authority and health authority at both officer and member level, informally and through such formal channels as the Joint Consultative Committee; and between individual members of voluntary organizations and providing establishments (eg between, say, the National Society for Deaf Children and the special schools or classes which many of the children will attend).

As for the future, in the light of the Warnock Committee's emphasis on the 'named person' and notwithstanding the attempt to dilute the potential usefulness of this function in the Education Act 1981, there is clearly a continuing role for the voluntary bodies, in extending some of the functions outlined above. It is to be hoped, however, that the voluntary organizations and local and health authorities in their dealings with them will avoid the very real danger that they will take on an advocacy role in individual casework, as has been seen to happen in the United States. The success of an authority's approach to and relationship with the voluntary sector may in future be indicated by the extent to which it can absorb and respond to the pressure for more and better services, and respond to their views about the provision available and thus retain a true partnership with the parents direct rather than through some pressure group which feels obliged to act on parents' behalf.

It is noticeable now, and is likely to be so in future, that the largest groups of children with special educational needs – those with moderate learning difficulties and the emotionally/socially disturbed, – do not have powerful voluntary organizations to press on their behalf, and perhaps more importantly to provide a mutually supportive group for parents. It is even more important in these cases that the school, whether it be a special or ordinary school, should be sensitive to this need and to the gap in the voluntary sector which has always been difficult to fill. Tribute should also be paid to the schools for the way in which they have attempted to do so in the past, frequently without the benefit of training or specific resources needed effectively to accomplish this difficult task.

Summary

This chapter has attempted to show how the approach to assessment of and provision for special educational needs, on the part of health services, personal social services and the voluntary sector have been inextricably linked historically and developmentally; and that they will remain so. The focus, inevitably and rightly, is upon the assessment of individual need and on provision matched as far as possible to that assessment. Contributions towards that assessment from many different disciplines will all have their special value, but may lead to conflict or confusion. It would be as easy, and misleading, to play down the importance of this point as it would be to underestimate the many professional, ethical, bureaucratic and personal factors which can, and demonstrably do from time to time, militate against the 'good interdisciplinary communication' on which so much stress has been laid here, reflecting the clear obligation, spelled out in DES Circular 1/83:

> 75. Inter-authority and inter-professional cooperation and collaboration are essential for effective assessment. The precise arrangements for cooperation and collaboration between health and local authorities will need to be worked out at the local level. All services should therefore review their patterns of work and agreed procedures which will avoid unnecessary duplication of work and delays, and which will help to ensure that the appropriate professionals can be involved quickly at any stage.

Whilst these comments were made in the narrow context of formal assessment, they are equally applicable to day-to-day working between the providing and supportive agencies, and crucially, between them and parents.

8 Teacher training and special educational needs

It is vital that all teachers should be alert to the existence of children with special educational needs. The Warnock Committee was clear-sighted and wise in pointing out in its planning assumptions that it is probable that about one child in six at any one time and up to one in five at some time in their school career will require some form of special educational provision. The great majority of such pupils will be found distributed amongst ordinary schools, though their incidence in any class or school will vary from time to time. But whether teachers are working with such pupils in special schools and units or in ordinary classes, whether teachers have a specific responsibility for pupils with special educational needs or encounter such pupils only occasionally or within larger groups; they must be conscious of the range and complexity of the needs they are likely to encounter and should be trained in ways which will allow them to respond in positive, optimistic and relevant ways to the situations they will meet. Only through training programmes, both initial and in-service, geared to the demands those situations create, can the process of integrating former special school pupils into ordinary schools be moved forward with sensible speed.

Training programmes of the range that will achieve so wide an objective will also be required for teachers of pupils with special educational needs in the sixteen–nineteen age band in further education. Though there are differences between the situations in schools and in further education, notably that a proportion of teachers in further education has had no initial training, there are features common to both sectors which will provide ground on which programmes of relevance can be based.

Teachers with specific responsibility for special educational needs will work either in special or in ordinary schools, though situations locally will vary according to the resources, both human and material, which LEAs are able to provide in special and in ordinary schools. It is impossible to conceive, however, a situation in which an LEA sees no need to maintain separate special provision. Children who are profoundly and/or multiply handicapped, those with severe emotional, behavioural and learning difficulties will continue to require support beyond the means of an ordinary school, and curricula which have been designed to meet their unusual or particular learning difficulties. But all teachers in the two to nineteen age group must be able to identify the special educational needs of their pupils, must be aware of how far they themselves can meet those needs and at what point they must seek the help of their specialist colleagues. In turn the specialists whose work is to coordinate provision in a school or in an authority should be prepared carefully for that role, and only experienced practitioners, familiar with the full ability range and with appropriate post-experience training should be given specific responsibility in special schools and for groups of pupils in ordinary schools. Similarly, staff advising teachers in ordinary schools which may have only a few pupils with special educational needs in their classes should be able to point to broad experience across the full ability range and post-experience training in the field. Subject specialist teachers should be able to take account of special educational needs in planning and developing specialist courses.

Such requirements are at present met by very few teachers. Indeed, many are ill-equipped to ensure that such needs are met. Some may have teaching qualifications but no specialist training for special needs; others may have specialist training but have not worked with pupils across the full ability range. The patterns of training must now be organized so as to prepare teachers more fully for their role in respect of pupils with special educational needs.

There is, at present, no widespread provision of initial training courses which pay special attention to pupils with special educational needs. A substantial option in the field may be offered but this detracts from study of the needs of the full range of pupils. Short intensive courses in special education may lead teachers to the false belief that special educational needs can only be met in special schools. All initial teacher training courses, including one-year courses, should aim to prepare students to be able to identify special needs as they arise at whatever age from very young to older pupils and to encourage students to adapt methods and materials to meet the needs of individual pupils. The role of the parent of the child with special educational needs should also be studied and ways of involving parents and establishing good working relationships with teachers and with schools should be developed. It would be very dangerous, moreover, for teachers not to be aware of the range of specialist services available to pupils and parents. Teachers operate as part of a multi-professional team and should be able to judge nicely the point at which they should seek specialist help and advice.

Such courses can no longer be the responsibility of an institution's 'special needs' tutors since an awareness of special educational needs must inform the work of all tutors if the requirements set out above are to be achieved. Teacher trainers may well lack the expertise required and a heavy burden will fall initially on the shoulders of those who do possess the necessary knowledge, skills and experience. Release of suitably qualified practising school teachers would be of value in accelerating the in-service training programmes of initial teacher training institutions. Without an integrated planning of provision to take account of special educational needs there will be little progress of value. Certainly, the CATE (Council for the Accreditation of Teacher Education) should look for speedy action in this field by institutions.

Such staff development programmes might include national and regional seminars and conferences, at which senior staff might consider, with HMI and LEA advisory staff, how initial training courses might meet criteria set by the Secretary of State. The contribution practising teachers might make is enormous. Individual institutions should set up in-house staff development programmes with outreach to regional centres and schools. The implications for specialist areas of teaching should receive detailed study. HMI might collect examples of best practice and publish them in a discussion document and support might be given to subject teacher associations or associations for teachers in remedial and special education to organize national and/or regional conferences. Appropriate research should continue to be encouraged and supported by the DES and, finally, institutions should seek, in making staff appointments, to enhance the range of expertise available to them.

Since there is insufficient time available in the initial training period to achieve more than minimal requirements without sacrificing other important elements, a heavy weight of responsibility rests on the providers of in-service training at local, regional and national level. The range of provision needed – from short courses for teachers whose work with special needs cases is occasional to higher degree work for coordinators and advisers – is enormous and though some good work is already being done, there is an urgent need for a national review of available courses and the filling of the obvious gaps which exist.

Local provision for meeting special educational needs will, inevitably, vary between LEAs but it is possible to envisage minimal standards if such needs are to be met adequately. LEAs should have advisers who are able to provide adequate in-service training for teachers and work with training institutions: administrators and headteachers who are able to organize a service capable of meeting the needs of the full ability range: specialist teachers in the field of special educational needs and a teaching force aware of the role it will be called upon to play. Movement towards this goal clearly involves local training programmes, long and short, full-time and part-time, which will enhance existing skills and implant new.

Neither time nor resources will allow so massive a programme to be completed quickly and clear priorities for the early stages should be set. Flexibility is valuable but it is sensible to remember that the existing base is rather narrow and prime 'target' groups can be identified to which the early courses should be directed. The headteacher of every school needs to be able to assume a full responsibility for ensuring that special educational needs are met, and management courses in future should include elements designed to help headteachers and senior staff in this responsibility. At the next level of operation every school should have easy access to a designated teacher who can identify the nature of individual special needs, devise strategies to overcome learning problems, contribute the development of a curriculm covering the full ability range and organize learning so that pupils with special educational needs have a clear access to that curriculum. Larger schools should have at least one such teacher; smaller schools would, perhaps, need to share an appointment or use LEA support and advisory services. The long-term aim should be to ensure that such teachers have followed a one-term, full-time course in line with the recommendations of DES Circular 3/83 on In-service Teacher Training Grant Schemes. Preparation of teachers to work with and guide their colleagues and to coordinate special needs work within schools is a fundamental requirement though too much should not be expected too soon of such courses.

LEAs will require the services of teachers who are acknowledged specialists in this field. Such specialists should be experienced teachers who have good experience of teaching in ordinary schools and have confirmed their interest in the work by undertaking a period of observation or supervised experience in the field. In this way their suitability for the work can be confirmed and they can then undertake the equivalent of one year's study, either full-time or part-time, leading to a recognized qualification. The modular regional diploma course jointly taught by Manchester University and Manchester Polytechnic offers an excellent example of a flexible part-time commitment for teachers. To gain best effect, such one-year training courses should provide opportunities for the teachers to acquire an understanding of how factors in the child, the family, the school and the community can interact to give rise to special educational needs. Knowledge of the development of children in all aspects, curriculum development and evaluation and the working of the full spectrum of educational and support services will enable teachers the more easily to meet special needs through effective curricular and general support. Collaboration with others and using the resources offered within the community are valuable strategies of which teachers should have detailed knowledge and they should be well versed in the role of planning and mounting local in-service training.

Each teacher engaged in such training should be given the chance to specialize still further by selecting a particular area of need such as emotional or behavioural disorders or working with a particular age group. Where there is a range of options in such specialisms the courses will be able to adjust more rapidly to the changing patterns of needs which will be discerned in the future. The field of special educational needs has few fixed points and change within it is rapid. A course concentrating on particular handicaps in isolation would deny teachers the benefit of working and exchanging experience with colleagues interested in other specialisms.

Regular in-service, up-dating courses, short in duration would keep teachers abreast of developments and would provide good opportunities for the further training of such teachers as have already acquired significant qualifications in work in satisfying special educational needs. Where subject specialists, whether from secondary or primary schools, undertake in-service training there should always be an element in the courses which deals with the curricular responsibilities of subject specialists towards the needs of pupils with special educational problems.

That teachers should become aware of the benefit to be gained from enlisting the aid of other agencies implies an equal responsibility on members of the supporting agencies to continue their professional training. Courses for senior officers in education, the NHS and the Social Services should have special needs elements.

Teachers' aides, nursery nurses and playgroup leaders should receive training in this field and those teachers and advisers and administrators who have a supervisory role should be given opportunity to acquire advanced diploma and degree qualifications in their chosen fields and should be encouraged to participate in applied research, particularly in the new technologies.

Let us now examine the value of specialist initial training courses which in the past have trained teachers for direct entry into specific types of special school. Of course the contribution of such teachers to their schools has been most beneficial but it is questionable whether such courses can justify a permanent place in future patterns of teacher training provision.

Between 1944 and 1954 as the special education service expanded, most teachers entering the special school service did so after training for teaching in ordinary schools. The Fourth Report of the National Council on the Training and Supply of Teachers advocated that teachers of handicapped children should first have experience in ordinary schools before in-service training prepared them for work with the handicapped. In 1971, following the decision to transfer the responsibility for the education of severely educationally subnormal in England and Wales to the education service and the concomitant need for more qualified teachers in ESN(S) schools, initial teacher training courses having a significant element connected with work with the severely handicapped were introduced. Qualifications obtained on such courses allowed those possessing them to work in either special or ordinary schools. The Warnock Committee noted a division of opinion between those who argued for more specific initial courses placing greater emphasis on the needs of the severely and multiply handicapped and those who believed in broader courses which did not narrow too much the focus of a teacher's work. The Warnock Committee believed that no new courses of a highly specialized nature should be established and that appropriate advanced in-service courses should be developed even though existing courses continued. By 1982 and the restructuring of initial teacher training which took place then, seven public sector institutions shared 95 BEd and postgraduate certificate of education places on specialist courses and some other institutions intended to offer teaching pupils with severe learning difficulties as an optional alternative to a specialism in mainstream primary education.

Since the Warnock Report the situation has continued to change and in June 1984 the Advisory Committee for the Supply and Education of Teachers (ACSET), in its advice to the Secretaries of

State, reached the following important conclusions. First, there was no longer a need to increase the number of trained teachers in schools for children with mild or severe learning difficulties [previously known as ESN(S) and ESN(M)] since 97 per cent of teachers in such schools possessed a recognized teaching qualification of some kind. What was now questionable was whether such teachers were *appropriately* trained for present and future needs. Second, the population of schools for pupils with learning difficulties is in the process of change. For example, the proportion of pupils with conditions such as Down's Syndrome is likely, because of better ante- and post-natal care, early screening and policies of integration into ordinary schools, to decrease. There is likely to be a corresponding increase in the proportion of the profoundly and multiply handicapped for whom programmes must be specially planned. The Advisory Committee argued the inappropriateness of initial training courses which concentrated on highly specialist fields where there is a shortage of posts and severe restrictions on the mobility and career prospects of those teachers who are employed. Third, the Secretary of State's criteria for the approval of all initial teacher training courses insist on preparation for the ordinary school. The courses for the mental handicap specialist cannot, argued the Advisory Committee, retain their special emphasis and, at the same time, satisfy the Secretary of State's criteria. As it is, too many specialists pursue too few vacancies scattered through the country and are forced to seek employment in ordinary schools where their training is not totally appropriate. Such a situation wastes expertise and frustrates the specialists who must acquire experience of the whole spectrum of ability before being able to deploy specialist skills fully and effectively.

Initial teacher training courses which specialize in the needs of children with severe learning difficulties were of value in the 1970s but are no longer appropriate to the circumstances of the 1980s and the 1990s. Equally, the few initial training courses which concentrated on the slow learner in the ordinary school are inappropriate in the current and future situation. Accordingly, ACSET recommended the phasing out of all such courses.

A classic example of the situation which so concerned ACSET presents itself in the four year degree course located in Manchester University's Department of Audiology and the Education of the Deaf. Here a study of audiology and two other academic subjects is combined with a course of teacher training and a specialist course in teaching the deaf. There is also a one-year postgraduate course leading to the award of the Certificate for Teachers of the Deaf which gives qualified teacher status whether taken as an initial training course or as a post-experience qualification. Both the undergraduate and graduate courses prepare students for employment in either ordinary or special schools. The question must be raised as to whether the four-year course with its essential focus on the techniques of teaching the deaf gives sufficient opportunity for students to acquire a real awareness of the full range of pupils either in ordinary schools or in schools for the deaf. Certainly graduates of this course will not easily compete with those who have had good experience of the full range of pupils and post-experience training in teaching the deaf. Still less can the one-year postgraduate certificate holders compete for posts. Though the conclusion inevitably reached is that the courses should be phased out it is vital that the expertise and facilities linked with them should be made available to enhance specialist in-service provision.

Phasing out such initial training courses will, of course, create a short-term shortage of teachers in the specialist areas of severe learning difficulties, slow-learning and teaching the deaf. That shortfall must be made good through in-service training led by key staff redeployed within institutions from initial to in–service training. The reservoir of expertise is sufficient to guarantee courses which will prepare trainers as well as specialist teachers and ensure a sufficient flow of suitably trained staff.

That redeployment should not be long delayed. Aware of the difficulties of persuading the CATE of the viability of specialist initial training courses, institutions would serve teachers and schools best by phasing out specialist initial training courses and replacing them by in-service courses which fit into a framework of national provision.

There is a good base on which to build such enhanced in-service provision and that base would be strengthened by the addition of resources released from courses no longer appropriate to present and future needs. Though tutors may be available as a part of such resources, it is possible that unreasonable demands may be made on institutions where such expertise is in short supply. Cooperation between institutions and authorities regionally should help to set up patterns of training to meet local needs. The provision of training courses for trainers will be required at national as well as regional level. A high priority to the in-service training of teachers to meet the special educational needs of pupils is vital and this has significant financial implications for the institutions and authorities involved. Not only are there the provision costs to consider but, additionally, the release costs of the teachers attending the courses. An immediate effort should be made to find increased funds nationally to cover release costs, and expansion of the teachers' in-service training grants scheme and the extension of eligibility for the pooling of salary release costs of the INSET pool to 100 per cent for designated courses would materially assist such a search.

It might be argued that LEAs would give high priority to in-service provision in the special needs area if mandatory requirements for specialist qualification were to be extended beyond the present limits of those teaching the blind, the deaf and the partially hearing. Such an extension however would have a counter-productive effect on the process of integration and it would be unrealistic to expect all teachers with children in their classes who have a range of disabilities to be multiply qualified. Indeed, a more powerful argument can be mounted for the withdrawal of mandatory requirements such as presently exist. A review of staffing standards in special schools and units and in some ordinary schools would give an adequate safeguard of professional standards – something which mandatory requirements have only partly achieved.

At present there is no clear indication of the target ratios for specialists acting as support teachers to ordinary schools or of the element of remission from normal teaching duties of teachers designated as teachers responsible for the coordination of work designed to satisfy special educational needs within a school. Discussion of these issues between central and local government and the teacher unions is a matter of urgency. In the meantime the monitoring of provision by HMI and LEAs and the remedying of staffing shortcomings thus identified will be useful. The Burnham Committee may have recommendations to make in the salary levels of teachers working either in support of schools or as teachers designated as responsible for special needs provision.

The further education sector offers a picture of great complexity; with a greater range of resources, it offers a wider variety of experiences than schools. Where school work is subject-based, further education work is course-based, though a greater flexibility in curriculum design in further education colleges is breaking this mould. Additionally, the special needs population in further eduction has, in recent years, been expanded by the shortage of jobs for school leavers, especially those with disabilities; by a recognition that in a further education setting an easier transition is made to the independence and responsibilities of adult life; and by the participation in college-based programmes of the MSC.

Teachers in further education must be able to recognize and cater for the special needs of their students to an extent not necessary a decade ago. There is an increased need, too, for colleges to cooperate with and draw upon the resources of the whole LEA rather than relying on their individual expertise and provision. A problem exists in that there is no initial training requirement in the further education sector – staff are appointed on the basis of academic or skills qualifications. Some staff have school teaching qualifications, some have the Certificate of Education (FE), and some have no formal training at all. In-service training, much of it in-house, is the main channel through which further education teachers will acquire a basic awareness training about special educational needs. The essential elements of such training – the identification of special needs, assessment of vocational and personal aptitudes of special needs pupils, the adaptation of curriculum and the use of specialized resources – are clear, but the best route by which training should be approached may well depend upon the degree of initial training the further education teacher possesses.

The best chances of success exist in setting up a national initiative for this increasingly urgent programme of awareness training. First, a series of regional seminars should promote the development of awareness training material appropriate to special educational needs in the sector. At least one tutor from each institution should attend such seminars. Work already in hand by HMI on a resource pack for further education teachers of students with moderate learning difficulties will offer useful guidance. Second, teachers in further education should be given full access to the specialist advisory services of LEAs and should contribute to those services. Institutions offering non-advanced provision will be most involved here, though some students on advanced courses may have sensory or physical handicaps.

Just as there are target groups among school teachers so there are target groups within the further education sector. A senior member of staff (Vice Principal or Head of Department) should ensure the proper resourcing and organization of special needs work and should be appropriately trained to do so. Another member of staff, where this is possible, should undertake a coordinating role in respect of special needs provision for students and in-service training for staff. Where specialist qualifications are not held by such teachers, opportunity should be given for early in-service training such as that recommended for coordinators in schools. Until an institution has, in the staff, a teacher who has a specialist qualification in the field, that institution should not plan special courses for those students with moderate or severe learning difficulties.

Demand for specialist training provision, depending as it does upon the collective identification of priorities by institutions, is not easy to assess, but LEAs and Regional Advisory Councils should undertake this exercise in consultation with other interested groups. The Regional Curriculum Bases of the Further Education Unit, the National Bureau for Handicapped Students and staff development groups of the MSC will help in the identification and assessment of training needs in further education. Further cooperation with schools will indicate areas where common provision is possible.

What is needed most urgently, however, is a fund of expertise in meeting special educational needs. On the shoulders of staff already possessing relevant qualifications will fall the task of developing and coordinating training on a regional basis. National courses of a high level for a smaller number of staff selected from institutions should be the responsibility of the DES who might also, over the next few years, keep the provision for special needs in further education under active scrutiny.

Further development will come as our collective awareness of the needs of pupils, students and those who teach them increases. That development will be all the more rapid as the data base, on which planning can be based, expands. At present there is inadequate information in central departments and local authorities on the range and distribution of need, on how those needs are and can be met and to what extent the teacher force is trained to deal with special educational needs.

9 Role of parents

The years since the implementation of the 1944 Education Act have seen a dramatic change in the involvement of parents in the education of their children. What has happened in these 40 years is a growing recognition by educators not only that parents have a voice, but also that that voice must be listened to if the education process is to succeed.

There have been two elements in this process. The first, which has been largely recognized by changes in legislation, is the awareness of the civil rights of parents. Although the 1944 Act spelt out the duties of parents to ensure that their children were adequately educated, it did not quite so clearly indicate any rights as to how that education was to be delivered. The 1980 Act created machinery through which parents could express preferences in the choice of schooling for their children and spelt out clearly how they might appeal against the decision of an authority to an apparently independent tribunal. That Act also gave parents the right of access to the Governing Bodies of schools by establishing their direct representation on those bodies. In doing so, it recognized the view expressed in the Taylor Report of 1977[1] which had indicated that governing bodies should be representative of all those with a major interest in running the school.

The second element might be seen as a more purely educational one and emerged from views about the influence and effect that parents both did have and should have upon the effectiveness of the education of their children. It had long been recognized that environmental factors were a significant influence on how children learn and that the support of parents in the process was important but it was perhaps the report of the Plowden Committee[2] that expressed more clearly a new recognition – that parents were themselves an important part of the teaching process.

This was a new dimension and one that has taken time to be fully absorbed. The role of adults other than teachers is perhaps still not totally a part of educational thinking but the success of experiments in paired reading – as reported at Belfield Primary School[3] and in other schemes – has shown that parents can offer more than support and that they can become crucial participants in the educational process. This element is not expressed quite so clearly in legislation but its effect on practice may ultimately be as significant. The survey of primary education in England conducted by Her Majesty's Inspectors of Schools between 1975 and 1977[4] reported on the involvement of parents:

> Parents help teachers in nearly a third of the 7 year old classes and in just over a fifth of 9 and 11 year old classes.

The report continues:

> In over three quarters of the classes where help was given parents assisted teachers in matters concerning the children's welfare and in the supervision of children on visits outside the school.

But more importantly:

> Teachers reported that parents were also involved in children's learning in the other two thirds of the classes where help was given.

This growth in both the rights of parents and in the acknowledgement of their importance in the educational progress is recognized most fully in the 1981 Education Act – legislation which places parents at the heart of the educational decision-making process.

Warnock and Parents

The influence of the Warnock Committee in preparing the ground is recognized in other chapters of this book but its recommendations on the role of parents, particularly the importance of acknowledging their rights in the process which determines the needs of their children, were clearly fundamental in framing the legislation. It is unfortunate that a further emphasis in Warnock – on the provision of appropriate help and support – is not recognized, perhaps because of its heavy resource implications.

The fundamental shift of attitude concerning parents was expressed clearly in the title of chapter 9 of the report – 'Parents as Partners'. The chapter begins:

We have insisted throughout this report that the successful education of children with special educational needs is dependent upon the full involvement of their parents: indeed, unless the parents are seen as equal partners in the educational process the purpose of our report will be frustrated.

The chapter goes on to develop the partnership theme.

We have chosen the title of this chapter deliberately, as expressing our view of the relationship between parents and members of the different professions who may be helping them at any time. It is a partnership, and ideally an equal one for although we tend to dwell upon the dependence of many parents on professional support, we are well aware that professional help cannot be wholly effective – if at all so – unless it builds upon the parents' own understanding of their children's needs and upon the parents' capacity to be involved.

The reports contrasts this concept with that of counselling which can too easily be seen as a one way process of enlightenment. Professionals are warned:

Parents can be effective partners only if professionals take notice of what they say and of how they express their needs, and treat their contribution as intrinsically important.

The Committee saw that the consideration of a child's special needs depends on a variety of perspectives and what the parent sees is as valid as what a professional sees. Indeed it will add to what others in the process see.

This chapter goes on to stress to the professionals involved with children with special needs that their relationship with parents is a reciprocal one.

It is of course very necessary that each professional – teacher, doctor, nurse, health visitor, social worker – should be knowledgeable about the application of his particular skills to children with special needs; it is no less important that he should exercise his skills in alliance with the parents and shape his contribution around the parents' own understanding of what is required.

Far from being merely a pious aspiration the report gave firm advice as to how the relationship between parents and professionals might be developed in four crucial areas:-

1. the assessment process;

2. information and advice;

3. involvement of parents with school;

4. the concept of the named person.

The Report recognized that parents are often the first people to appreciate that a child might have special needs. One aspect of this was the need to ensure that all prospective parents should be able to acquire a knowledge of child development. The corollary was that professionals were enjoined to take seriously the concerns expressed by parents about the development of their children. A research project undertaken on behalf of the Committee had in fact demonstrated the difficulties which many parents had had in convincing professionals in the field that problems existed.

The first criterion of an effective assessment process was seen to be the early involvement of parents. The assessment process needed information which only parents could supply and the educational programme which proceeded out of assessments required their cooperation. There were cases where early involvement might not be in the child's best interests but the report, curiously, did not specify what might occasion a departure from the rule. Parents should not only be involved in the assessment – they should be informed of the results. This seems obvious – but was worth stating. The report suggested that as soon as a school proposed to use outside advice about a child, parents should be consulted. The procedure which existed for assessment when the report was written was not one which deliberately excluded parents but there was no statutory requirement to include them. Circular 2/75 had introduced the Special Education Procedures which moved influence in the assessment process away from doctors and located it with psychologists. The circular had encouraged early parental consultation and stated that: 'Parents normally recognize the need for special education for their child provided they are involved in discussion from an early stage.'

However, this presupposed a situation in which parents were to be persuaded of the rightness of the assessment rather than be involved in it as contributors. Gray, in a study published as an occasional paper by the Division of Education and Child Psychology of the British Psychological Society[5], showed that the involvement of parents revolved around reporting their agreement. That professional practice was to involve parents is shown by the very few parents who resorted to the appeals procedures available to them but there was a very strong element of persuasion rather than a canvassing of information and views. The report considered the Special Education assessment procedure and pointed out that parents had no significant involvement in it. The existing forms merely provided opportunities for the head teacher and educational psychologists to record the parents' wishes. However, the Warnock report recommended: 'Whoever refers the child for multi-professional assessment should inform the parents as soon as the SE procedure has been initiated and should give them a form on which to make their own statement about their child's needs.'

It suggested the kind of questions that parents might be asked:

> This form should contain questions abouts its significant events in their child's life as well as more general questions such as: what do you think is your child's main problem? what are his main strengths and special interests? what sort of special help do you think he needs? In addition, the form should ask for details of any professional consultations that have taken place about the child, and should give the parents opportunity to indicate whether or not they have any objections to the consultants being approached for further information.

How is this parental involvement to be achieved? The report recognized that parents needed information, advice and support if they were to play their new role fully. There were four ways in which information could be provided. First, parents whose children had a handicapping condition should be taken into professional confidence as soon as possible, and, at that stage, given information about the facilities and supporting services available. Second, it was suggested that resource centres on handicap should be established with facilities for parents to consult the available literature. Third, LEAs were recommended to produce and keep up-to-date a handbook for their areas showing the range of special educational provision available. Fourth, individual schools should be required to produce their own handbooks describing the facilities available in them.

Similarly, advice and support could come in a variety of ways. Such support might be practical – the provision of transport or of aids. It might be support through home/school liaison teachers or peripatetic teachers working primarily with under fives. Emphasis was placed on the role of voluntary organizations and particularly on the role that self-help groups of parents might take on in support-ing each other. Such groups were seen as reducing the isolation of parents and enabling them to learn from each other about the kind of help and encouragement that could be given to their children.

Above all, the report recognized that without guidance it would be difficult for parents to negotiate the complex support systems that existed or would be created if the recommendations of the Act were implemented. To make such guidance available, each parent whose child had special needs should have a 'named person'. This person would be a single point of contact for the parent whose main function was to introduce them to services or to ensure that any concern which might be present about a child's development was followed up. Who this person was would change according to the age and need of the child. Initially the health visitor would be appropriate, then the headteacher and ultimately the specialist careers officer. It was important that the named person should act as a link between these various stages or when a child moved from one area to another. Although the named person was seen as having a counselling responsibility, the concept of this person acting as an advocate in the interests of the parents of a child was not developed. It was recognized also that parents might neeed access directly to the officers of an education authority who were responsible for conducting the assessment who might, if need be, suggest a change in the named person.

The 1981 Education Act

The 1981 Education Act is largely silent on the subjects of curriculum provision or the organization of special education, although Section 2 lays upon education authorities the duty to secure that, where possible, children with special educational needs are educated in the ordinary school. Here parents have an important right – any such integration must be in accordance with their wishes. But for parents, the most significant sections of the Act are those which give them a wide ranging involvement in the assessment process.

An authority may assess a child under the age of two only with the consent of parents, (Section 6(1)). Under Section 10 of the Act an Area or District Health Authority which forms the opinion that a child has special educational needs must inform the parents of its opinion and must put the parents in contact with any particular voluntary organization which is likely to be able to give advice or assistance. If a LEA identifies a child over the age of two years who is judged to require an assessment they must first (Section 5) notify the parents and inform them of the procedure to be followed, of the name of an officer of the authority from whom further information may be obtained, and of their right to make representations and submit written evidence. If the authority then decides to continue with the assessment the parents must be notified and informed of the authority's reasons. If the authority decided at any time not to continue with an assessment the parents must be informed and if ultimately the authority decided after assessment that they are not required to determine any special educational provision, the parents must be informed both of that decision and of their right to appeal against it to the Secretary of State. A parent may, (Section 9), request an assessment or a reassessment after six months of an original assessment and the authority must comply with that request unless they are satisfied either that the original request is unreasonable or that an assessment is inappropriate.

In making its assessment, the authority must take into account the representations or evidence submitted by or at the request of the parent (Regulations-Section 8). When requesting advice from other professionals the authority must ensure that they have a copy of the representations or evidence from the parents (Regulations-Section 4).

When the authority has drafted its statement of a child's special educational needs it must submit a copy of that proposed statement to the parents of the child, (Section 7), and the statement will contain as appendices copies of all the advice that has been submitted to the authority (Regulations Section 10). At this stage the authority must also inform parents of their rights to make representations about the draft (Section 7). Parents may require the authority to enable them to meet an officer and they may require the authority, following that meeting, to arrange further meetings to enable the parents to discuss the relevant advice with the appropriate person or persons (Section 7). The statement must be accompanied by a notice in writing of the name of a person to whom the parents may apply for information and advice about the child's special educational needs.

Following any such representations, the authority may then issue a statement but must at the same time inform parents of their right to appeal against the special educational provision specified (Section 7). The appeal is not against the assessment of need but is related only to the way in which the LEA propose to respond to that need. The LEA must create the machinery for enabling parents to appeal and the appeal committee may remit the case to the authority who must then reconsider it and inform the parents of their decisions. Finally, if the parents do not agree with either the decision of the appeals committee or the reconsideration of the authority they may appeal to the Secretary of State.

The administrative procedure which the Act describes is obviously complex and to many parents may present a frighteningly bureaucratic appearance, but Circular 1/83 which was published to coincide with the implementation of the Act stresses throughout the need to establish good relationships. The circular refers to the Warnock concept of parents as partners and adds:

> Assessment should be seen as a partnership between teachers, other professionals and parents in a joint endeavour to discover and understand the nature of the difficulties and needs of individual children. Close relations should be established and maintained with parents and can only be helped by frankness and openness on all sides.

Paragraph 36 lays a further stress on the crucial importance of the relationship between parents and professionals. This paragraph hints at the changing role of the professional advisers since: 'Parental involvement in assessment provides the opportunity to reach an agreed understanding of the nature of a child's learning difficulties.'

If that understanding is to be agreed, it is obvious that the parents' views are critical. The Circular develops the Act's concept of the named person and again in paragraph 52 emphasizes not only that the person should be knowledgeable but also that: 'They should be able to establish good relations with parents.'

The Circular describes and emphasises a concept of good practice which the bureaucratic procedure of the Act might be seen to threaten. Nevertheless, the legislation by giving additional rights to parents changes dramatically their relationship both to the professionals who give advice and to the LEA which puts that advice into practice. If the spirit of legislation is implemented in its practice then the parent becomes a major determinant in the process of defining the child's needs and a major influence in how those needs should be met.

These rights may be seen in three ways. First, the parent has the right to express a choice not only about the style of provision for the child but about whether or not an authority should begin to determine a child's needs through the process of assessment. Ultimately, through the appeal process, the decision rests with the Secretary of State but the parents do have access to the process of decision-making. Second, the parents have the right to see the information on which the decision concerning the child is made. It may always have been good practice to involve parents and to discuss reports with them but an authority in the past could maintain the confidentiality of the advice given. Now that advice is public and may be and often is questioned by parents. Third, the views, the representations, and evidence submitted by the parents stand equally alongside the reports of the professionals. Indeed, the

parents' views and evidence precede their statements and professionals are required by law to take them into account.
That these rights exist in the legislation is one thing but to enable
parents to gain access to them is quite another. The complexity of
the assessment process could be used by authorities to prevent
access unless there is a recognition of the role of parents and a
subsequent recognition that authorities have a duty to enable them
to fulfil that role. It is too easy for parents to feel that the
cumbersome process of assessment has taken over. It may be seen to
be under the control of the authority or even worse be under no
control at all. Parents need to have their views clearly stated, understood and respected. They need to be given information, not only
about the procedures of the Act but about the nature of their child's
needs and the variety of provision available to meet those needs. The
best support that an authority can give to parents is to recognize and
respond to the different roles parents have in relation to their
children's education.

Parents are, first of all, home teachers. Of all roles this is the most
natural. Parents teach their children the skills of daily living, they
serve as models for appropriate behaviour and by listening to and
talking with their children they make the most of the environment
around them. Parenting needs to be recognized as a skilled job.
When a child has a disability parents may need additional help in
understanding how, in a warm and stable home, children may learn
alternative ways of coping with their problems.

Home/school liaison teachers, voluntary bodies and self help
parents' groups can be important and an authority should seek to
create a climate in which such groups can flourish.

Second, with their new place in the assessment process, parents
can become important as information specialists. They have the
opportunity to observe their children in a sustained way which is not
available to the other partners in the assessment process whose
knowledge of the child is inevitably based on short but intensive
periods. In this role parents can gather valuable knowledge about
their child's development and patterns of behaviour. They can
recognize problems and gauge successes. Much of this can be done
intuitively but parents should be helped to look for the signs which
are significant. They may also need help to articulate knowledge
which they have in order that others can share it with them.
Whether this information is passed on at case conferences, discussions with pyschologists or teachers, or in written evidence, there
is an obligation to professionals both to create a receptive climate

and to provide parents with the vocabulary to describe the child's progress. Parents need to be aware that the situation in which they find themselves can be both frightening and confusing and that this may inhibit them from talking freely. Confidence in the professionals can be achieved if they show themselves prepared to listen and prepared to respond.

Third, parents are case managers in the sense that they share a responsibility for reaching appropriate decisions about their children. They cannot do this unless they have all the information which others in the system have and that information needs to be presented in a comprehensible way. Parents may need advice about handling the information which they are given. This may be on a personal level but it may also be a matter of providing them with advice about the need to store and record information and decisions and the need to respond to letters and documents. The documents presented should make the options available clearly and should spell out the steps which parents can take.

This role merges into the fourth role which parents have which is to act as an advocate for their child. This can be, for a local authority, the most threatening of all parental roles because it may bring the parent into conflict with other pressures, particularly the authority's own views of the need for an efficient use of resources. Nevertheless, an authority must recognize its duty to provide parents with the information about their rights, the policy of the authority and the provision available which will enable them to argue for proper decisions for their children. It may be argued that there are occasions when the needs of the child are not well represented by the parents and when indeed their concept of those needs is at odds with what others honestly see as best for the child. At this point the appeals procedure can be used constructively to establish an independent judgement of the most appropriate course of action.

Can parents effectively fulfil all these demanding roles? Many do but many also find the procedures too cumbersome and the pressures of daily living with a child with difficulties too demanding. The reaction of parents in this situation may be either to allow decisions to be made in which they take no real part or, on the other hand, to regard all decisions as being made by a hostile and alien body. There is a case for extending the Warnock concept of the named person, which is weakly reflected in Section 7 of the Act, to the creation of a key worker. Such a worker might be independent of the authority but knowledgeable about the authority's system and charged with the duty of enabling parents to express their views, to contribute information and to play an important part in the process of a child's education. The key worker would preferably be known to the family and trusted by them, and equipped with particular skills in counselling. This could be a role for voluntary agencies to develop in conjunction with an authority, given the pressures on resources.

The particular need for this role is most clearly seen at the stage when the assessment procedures involve the parents of very young children. The Warnock Report had stressed the need for sensitivity when parents might well be suffering from the mixed emotions of shock and anger which the birth of a severely handicapped child can given rise to. The 1981 Act recognized this and required health authorities to inform parents of appropriate voluntary agencies at the stage when they are bringing to the attention of the education authority that the child may have special educational needs. At this stage then, parents might be counselled by a doctor, contacted by a voluntary society, be requested by an education authority to submit representations and evidence about their child and be visited by social services, a teacher and an educational psychologist in the process of constructing their advice about the child. All of these visitors will be well meaning and sympathetic – but there must be some sympathy for the parent faced with such a phalanx of the knowledgeable. None of them can clearly be seen to have the interests of the parent at heart except perhaps the voluntary agency.

What is suggested is an intermediary in the system – not necessarily another teacher but one of the existing group charged specifically to act initially as a go-between, explaining the process, clarifying ambiguities, helping to prepare evidence and, on occasions, speaking directly for the parents. This role would have to be clearly recognized by the professionals in the process who might need to be less jealous than usual of their professional territory. For some parents the key worker might only have an initial importance as they clarified for themselves both their own feelings and the nature of the system. Other parents might see the key worker as having an importance throughout the child's school career.

Who should play this role is less easy to decide. On the one hand is the need for the key worker to be seen as independent of the various authorities while on the other is the need for the worker to have both information about the system and access to those wielding power within it. A voluntary agency would play this role and parents can find mutual support valuable but the workers would need training in a range of social work and counselling skills. The Warnock Report recognized the contribution of health visitors and they also have the advantage of the most immediate access to parents. In some authorities, education welfare workers have extended into this social work role but they may be seen by parents in some instances to be too closely aligned with those aspects of the education authority which are regarded as punitive. Educational psychologists or peripatetic teachers may have many of the necessary skills but can again be perceived to be too closely linked to the system. The multiplication of professional roles is perhaps already too apparent – any additions to it may be unwelcome, particularly the creation of a whole new category of key workers, and it might be preferable to equip an existing participant in the process with the necessary skills of care and detachment rather than to create an additional post.

Indeed, it is certain that local authorities would not have the resources to make appointments of this kind but this should not prevent them from recognizing the need to bring to the administrative process of assessment patience and humanity and to recognize that an efficient system is one which values the contribution that parents make to the education of their children.

References

1. *A New Partnership For Our Schools*, Taylor Report, HMSO, 1977
2. *Children And Their Primary Schools*, Plowden Report, HMSO 1966
3. *The Belfield Reading Project*, A. Jackson & P Hannon, Belfield Community Council, 1981
4. *Primary Education In England*, HMI Report. HMSO 1979
5. *Are We Ready For The Statement?*, P J Gray. Occasional Papers – British Psychological Society, 1984

10 Northern Ireland, Scotland and Wales

Special education in Northern Ireland

The world of special education in Northern Ireland is currently in the midst of the most radical and fundamental changes which have affected the provision for children with special educational needs since the 1947 Education Act (NI) provided the original statutory basis for such provision. The Education Order (NI) 1984, which passed through Parliament in September of that year, has created a new framework for special educational provision which broadly parallels that established by the 1981 Act in Great Britain. Its emphasis is on the determination of special needs rather than the categorization of handicap, on the matching of need to provision, on statutory parental rights to involvement rather than on voluntary consultation and on the principle of integration within 'ordinary' schools. The Order also gives young persons the right to have their special needs met in an educational setting up to the age of nineteen years. However, the detailed arrangements for implementing the new legislation in the context of Northern Ireland have yet to be worked out and the Statutory Rules and Orders published, so that it is still too early to assess the impact of this legislation on children, parents, teachers and schools. We may, however, hope that the delay of three years in bringing forward such legislation in the province may prove valuable in allowing us to learn from mainland experience. January 1986 is the target date for the implementation of the new arrangements on the ground. Given the similar attitude of government here to the funding of such major changes as applied in Great Britain in 1981, namely that they should not lead to significantly increased expenditure on special education, it is unlikely that these changes will satisfy all the aspirations of parents. Nor will they lead to the comprehensive and individualized provisions which the proponents of such fresh initiatives in special education desired in pressing for new legislation, unless the resources are provided to match needs. Nevertheless, the legislation is a major and welcome step forward.

Hard on the heels of this Education Order has come a statement, made by the Minister of State for Education for the province in January 1985, that further legislation will soon be introduced to provide for the transfer of responsibility for special care schools from the Health and Social Services Boards, which currently administer them, to the Education and Library Boards. The position of the special care schools, which provide for the more severely mentally handicapped, was reviewed in 1972 when, on the mainland, they had been transferred to the education authorities. At that time, however, in Northern Ireland it was decided to retain such provision within the Health and Social Services field. Education authorities continued to be required to determine children needing the specialized educational, therapeutic and care provision of such schools as 'unsuitable for education at school'. Over the last thirteen years when the province has been governed directly from Westminster, the disparity between these arrangements and those in Great Britain has been the subject of much debate and dissatisfaction, especially amongst parents. A joint working group of the two Civil Service departments concerned, the Department of Education for Northern Ireland (DENI) and the Department of Health and Social Services (DHSS), was established some two years ago to review the situation once more. This group embarked upon a wide ranging consultative process in which the Education and Library Boards, individually and through the collective voice of their Association, (the provincial equivalent of CLEA), were in the forefront of seeking a change which would give children, parents and teachers access, as of right, to the full range of educational resources. They also wished to put an end to the description, however qualified, of some children as 'unsuitable for education'. The Minister's statement has now ended speculation regarding this issue. The Education and Library Boards and the Health and Social Services Boards have been advised that the transfer will take place in 1987. The two Civil Service departments have commenced the process of detailing the arrangements for transfer and the education and health authorities have also begun discussions to ensure that the specialized services of the two types of authority can continue to be available to severely disabled children and young persons, in a coordinated and integrated manner, after the transfer. This will be no easy task. The issues of resource transfer, of day and out-of-school care coordination and of provision for life beyond school age will require most careful and sympathetic handling in a spirit of cooperation and teamwork.

The statutory framework

It will be apparent that the framework for the administration of educational, health and social services in Northern Ireland differs somewhat from that in the rest of the UK. This has had some bearing on the special education scene in the province. Up to the reorganization of local government in 1973 all these services were operated by committees of the six County and two City Councils in Northern Ireland. The committees were partly independent of the Councils and related closely to the separate Ministries of the Northern Ireland Parliament, which had devolved powers for these services. Nevertheless they were under the umbrellas of Councils which had statutory powers to operate both sets of services and could exercise a coordinating role. In 1973 a major reorganization of local government took place. The eight Councils referred to above were replaced by 26 District councils, none of which (with the exception of Belfast City) would have been of sufficient size to administer regional services such as health, education or social services. Indeed the functions given to the new District Councils were quite minor. Instead separate ad hoc Boards were formed for Health and Social Services on the one hand and for Education, along with the public library service, on the other. Each Board administers the area of several District Councils (except for the Belfast Education and Library Board whose area is the same as the Belfast City Council). The membership of these bodies comprises a minority of democratically elected councillors along with representatives of churches and the professions served by the Boards and with ministerial appointees. Apart from the Eastern Health and Social Services Board, the area of which covers most of that administered by both the Belfast and the South Eastern Education and Library Boards, the two sets of Boards have broadly contiguous boundaries. However there is no linking or coordinating mechanism at a unitary council level to ensure that the full range of services which the two types of Board can provide is applied effectively to individual institutions or clients. Issues of conflicting priority have arisen from time to time, especially in relation to the scope and allocation of therapeutic, paramedical and medical services to children in schools, all of which services are supplied by the Health and Social Services Boards. Similarly, information flow between the two sets of authority is not always as complete as it should be. The most effective inter-service arrangements which have emerged within this structure have been at local level. These have arisen from the close day-to-day working relationships between individual educational psychologists, education welfare officers, peripatetic teachers of the handicapped and headteachers of special schools on the one hand and clincial psychologists, medical officers, social workers, speech, language, physio and occupational therapists and heads of special care schools on the other. From time to time concerns regarding district coordination of services have been brought to the two types of individual Board by District Councillors. In general however, coordination of policy and basic approach has been lacking or else has appeared only in relation to major policy decisions at Civil Service departmental level.

Central and local government

Apart from the absence of multi-functional Council authorities, certain other differences between the Northern Ireland Education and Library Boards and English or Welsh LEAs exist. Education and Library Boards have no powers to raise their own finance through rates. Nor have they County Councils to do this on their behalf and to allocate funds to them. Instead they are funded directly by DENI from funds raised by a provincial rate, supplemented by direct grants from Westminster. DENI is therefore the body directly accountable to Parliament for educational expenditure in Northern Ireland and it discharges this accountability through a range of detailed statutory controls on the actions of the Boards and through powers to approve Board decisions on policy and provision. DHSS exercises similar controls on the Health and Social Services Boards. Thus the Boards have had to develop a day-to-day working relationship with central government which applies not only to broad policy areas but also to much of the detail of action in the special education field. Whilst an intimate relationship of such a kind between central and local government can have important benefits in improving communications, coordinating development and avoiding duplication, it can also from time to time produce tensions within the service. On occasions local initiative can be frustrated by the delays often inherent in such dual arrangements.

School authorities

In addition to the major division between responsibility for special schools and for special care schools already referred to, within the broad scope of the Education and Library Boards' responsibilities there exists a number of other quasi-autonomous school authorities in the province. Several of these are involved in special education provision. The Education and Library Boards directly manage only controlled schools (ie LEA schools in England and Wales). The vast majority of special schools fall within this category and are managed by the Boards through School Boards of Governors appointed by them and comprising members of the Board, parents' representatives, assistant teacher members (from 1985) and representatives of the local community. Since 1968, however, a statutory provision has existed whereby the managers of any voluntary (ie private) school could seek 'maintained' status for the school. Such status meant that 100 per cent of the school's running costs was paid by the Education and Libraries Board and 85 per cent of the cost of capital development by DENI. Nearly all the schools provided by the Roman Catholic Church Authorities have, by now, been admitted to such status. These include three special schools – one for deaf and two for ESN Children. There is also one non-denominational maintained special school – for deaf and blind children. Whilst, in return for such funding, the Boards have a one-third representation on the Boards of Governors of such maintained schools, they are not directly responsible for the management of them and do not have control over what is taught in them. In the field of special education this aspect has been particularly important as, in addition to the three Roman Catholic maintained special schools already referred to, there is a considerable number of special classes in or special units attached to 'ordinary' maintained schools. These, along with their controlled school equivalents, have been a major feature of special educational provision in the province for many years. As they come under the management arrangements relevant to the parent school, this provision in maintained schools is also not directly under the control of the Boards although the Boards place the children in such schools and units. Again effective partnership arrangements between the Boards and the maintained school authorities have been vital to the successful operation of such a system, especially as the Boards have an overarching statutory reponsibility for the adequacy of special educational provision in their areas. Also, through their educational psychology services, the Boards are wholly responsible in law, for assessment of children and subsequently for the provision of the necessary special educational treatment.

Inspectors, advisers and support services

In view of the diversity of school authorities, DENI has retained responsibility for the inspection of schools and teachers. In the context of special education, DENI inspectors have rights of access to all special schools and special classes/units, whether under controlled, maintained or voluntary management. With the agreement of the Health and Social Services Boards, DENI inspectors since 1978 have also inspected the special care schools. The Education and Library Boards do not have an inspectorial role but, in supplementation of the critical support of the DENI inspectorate, they have developed an advisory and supportive role towards staff and curriculum development. In special education this advisory role has been carried out by educational psychologists, by the team leaders of the Boards' peripatetic teaching services and by general advisers and school support service field officers employed by the Boards. Area Board advisory and support service personnel have been welcomed into their schools by the voluntary and maintained school authorities and, in recent years, have also been involved with teachers in the special care schools. The full range of in-service training provision for teachers, organized jointly by DENI and the Education and Library Boards, has been made available to teachers in all special schools, units and classes including those in the special care schools. This kind of day-to-day working arrangement, irrespective of legal obstacles, is typical of the education scene in Northern Ireland. Through this role, the Boards have played an increasing part in influencing the form of the curriculum for children with special educational needs and the methodology employed to implement curricular programmes. In agreement with voluntary and maintained school authorities and DENI, Boards have implemented a number of curricular initiatives in special education. Particular examples are in relation to behavioural problems and to truancy amongst teenagers. Teamwork between the Boards and DENI has been particularly important in securing resource support for initiatives of this sort, as DENI retains control over the finance for full-time teachers' salaries and has the final approval of the allocation of full-time teachers to individual schools. The ability of the Boards to supplement the quota of full-time teachers by part-time staff from within their own resources has also been an important feature of such developments, adding useful flexibility to arrangements. The Boards also employ and pay for the non-teaching staff in controlled and maintained schools. These include classroom attendants and assistants, houseparents and other care staff in special education.

The development of special education in Northern Ireland

Geographical considerations

The above description sets the legal and political framework within which special education has developed. It is, however, important, in examining this development, to take into account certain geographical and demographic features of the province. Northern Ireland is a relatively compact region and it is possible within a weekly boarding framework to provide many specialist services for the province as a whole at a single location. Set against this factor the total population, at little over 1½ million people, is small. Over one-third of this population is concentrated in the greater Belfast area and, except for this area, along with N. Down and Londonderry, the population is widely scattered and generally at a low density. This has created problems of viability for specialist facilities in many local areas outside Belfast. With a relatively small total population, highly specialist educational institutions are not viable within Northern Ireland, for example those providing for specialized types of sight or hearing impairment, for severe epileptics or for a range of disabilities beyond school leaving age. In these fields, boarding places at institutions in Great Britain or in the Republic of Ireland have been paid for by the Boards. There is however very comprehensive provision within Northern Ireland to meet most forms of special education needs.

Historical background

As on the mainland, much of the early provision for children with specialist educational needs in the province arose, after the second world war, from the development of charitable institutions whose original emphasis had, perhaps through necessity, been more on care than on education. In these, paramedical and educo/therapeutic services were combined with residential care from early childhood through into adulthood. Examples of such were the institutions run by the Cripples Institute in Belfast and Bangor, the Institutes for the Deaf and the Blind at Jordanstown and the Malcolm Sinclair Trust for the Physically Handicapped in Belfast. In the 1920s and 1930s, however, the Northern Ireland Parliament had developed arrangements for the transfer of schools established by voluntary bodies (mainly the protestant churches at that time) into state management. These guaranteed the originators of such schools a continuing involvement in the management of the state run schools through the appointment of their representatives on to management committees. Thus in the years following the 1947 Education (NI) Act, arrangements of this type were made by the then Ministry of Education to allow the school parts of institutions for handicapped persons to be transferred to the education committees. This assurance of continuing influence and involvement proved of great value in encouraging transfer of schools and many of the schools set up by charities were so transferred and continue in existence as controlled special schools today. The later 'maintained' school arrangements described previously enhanced the opportunities for voluntary schools to obtain public funding and to come within the public sector of education. Today all special schools are within the broad 'state' sector, with either controlled or maintained status.

Development in the early years

The 1947 Act defined for the first time categories of handicap and laid on the Education Committees the responsibility for securing adequate provision, either within their own areas or by sending children to other education authorities, for each of these types of handicap. A similar responsibility was laid on the County and Borough Health Committees in respect of children referred to them by the Education Committees as being 'unsuitable for education at school', though the special care schools to which such children were usually sent, were, in fact, originally established by the NI Hospital Authority. Given that schools providing for the more traditionally recognized forms of handicap referred to earlier already existed, in the early years after 1947 the Education Committees concentrated on making provision for the educationally subnormal children who had been defined for the first time in that Act. A considerable number of special ESN schools was established in the major towns in the province in the 1950s. These provided a mixture of residential facilities for children coming from distant and scattered rural communities and day attendance facilities for children from the more immediate surrounding areas. In parallel with these specialist facilities at widely spaced major town locations, from the outset ESN children with relatively minor disabilities, as well as those with lesser physical handicaps, were retained within the 'ordinary' school system. Remedial classes and groups were established in primary and secondary schools from 1947. Special class allowances, payable on top of the normal Burnham Scales for teachers in 'ordinary' schools, were introduced to assist with the recruitment of suitably trained and experienced teachers to teach such classes and groups. The Boards and the voluntary school authorities employed a considerable number of full and part-time remedial teachers for this purpose. Many physically handicapped children have also been able to attend ordinary schools in their own communities through the provision by the Boards of classroom attendants and of specialist equipment. The integration of handicapped children into ordinary schools has therefore been a feature of special education in the province from long before the 1984 Order added legal force to such a concept. Teams of peripatetic remedial teachers and of teachers of the hearing impaired have also been employed by the Boards to assist with provision in the smaller rural schools. These work in both controlled and maintained schools. They also undertake an advisory role in assisting teachers of special classes and groups in ordinary schools in relation to the curriculum and methodology for dealing with pupils with disabilities.

Assessment and placement

Decisions as to whether a child should attend the local primary/ secondary school or should go to a special school or unit, although formally recorded by the Education and Library Boards, have in general been taken through a close consultative process, involving the parents, the headteachers of both types of school and the area educational psychologists. Rarely have decisions been taken without the parents' full support and there has been little evidence over the years of significant conflict between parents and education authorities about placements. It may well be that the close involvement of the heads of the schools in the process and the concentration on local level consultations and working arrangements has been a major factor in avoiding conflict. The general informality of the proceedings may also have been a factor. Concern has been expressed lest the greater centralization and formality implicit in following the 1981 Act arrangements of England and Wales may cause more conflict than it will cure. Similar processes have been involved at the interface between special education and special care, though it would be fair to say that, especially in more recent years, the formal processes involved in this area have led to more parental dissatisfaction and disquiet than in other parts of the special education scene. There remains a strong emotional objection to declaring formally that a child is 'unsuitable for education at school'. It is hoped, that the forthcoming transfer of responsibility for education in special care schools to the Education and Library Boards will remove this.

The move away from residential placements

The existence of residential special schools for ESN children and the later development of such schools for maladjusted children rapidly proved to be of benefit to the Welfare and Social Services Departments in arranging residential placements for children in their care, but with educational problems. However, over the last ten years the whole role of residential provision for children with special educational needs has been reassessed. In particular the taking of children with severe but non-pschiatric behavioural problems into residential establishments has been, for the most part, discontinued. In parallel with this review the number of district special units attached to local primary and secondary schools has been increased. These have been mainly for children with learning difficulties (ESN) and for partially hearing children. More recently educational guidance units have been established in Londonderry and Coleraine for children with truancy and/or behavioural problems. The opening of the Jaffe Centre in Belfast has provided a separate day attendance school for problem children from some of the most difficult inner city areas, with specialist programmes aimed at rehabilitating them to normal schooling.

Several assessment and diagnostic units for children of pre-school age have also been developed, attached in some cases to primary schools and in others to special schools. In the light of these developments the number of children attending many of the special schools on a residential basis has steadily declined to the point where, by now, the vast majority of the children attend on a day basis. Where necessary they are provided with special transport from their homes in the surrounding districts. Special schools are also starting to develop more as resource and outreach centres for ordinary schools in their area. The 1984 Education Order may give impetus to these developments. Short term withdrawal placements for children with behavioural or, indeed, learning problems may become more common. Teachers from special schools may become increasingly involved in running courses for children with special needs in ordinary schools and colleges of further education or in assisting their colleagues in these schools and colleges with the development of programmes for children with disabilities.

Teacher training

Mainstream teacher training in the province, as opposed to in-service, has always been a responsibility of DENI rather than of the Education and Library Boards. Full-time courses were established shortly after the 1947 Act at each of the province's Teacher Training Colleges for students wishing to teach in special schools. Up to 1962 a one year end-on addition to the basic three year course led directly to a Certificate in Special Education for such students. This course dealt mainly with remedial teaching. Trainees wishing to specialize in other fields of handicap had, in general, to seek such specialist training outside the province. Since 1962 the initial training of teachers specifically for special education has been discontinued. Today the three and four year B Ed courses at the Teacher Training Colleges and the end-on post graduate Diploma and Certificate in Education courses at Queens University and the University of Ulster all contain a component on teaching children with disabilities. All prospective teachers in the province must follow one of these courses. Additional specialist training for teachers of children with special educational needs is only available to experienced teachers, in the form of post service courses – normally the one-year Diploma in Special Education – run by the Teacher Training Colleges and by the newly created University of Ulster at Jordanstown. As already mentioned, a range of specialist short courses and school-focussed in-service training activities is provided in partnership between the Boards and DENI using the resources of the Higher Education Institutes, the Inspectorate of DENI, the Boards' advisory services and local teachers. The Boards' teachers' centres play an important role in this provision. However, many students wishing to specialize in particular handicaps continue to obtain their teacher training in Great Britain. The Department of Health and Social Services for a number of years provided training courses, firstly at Muckamore Hospital and then at the former Northern Ireland Polytechnic, for teachers in or wishing to enter special care schools. In 1980 these were discontinued. Access to in-service training organized by DENI and the Boards has been offered since then to teachers working in special care schools. The transfer of these schools in 1987 to the Education and Library Boards may necessitate a major review of training arrangements for teachers working in them.

School leavers

Since 1947 the school leaving age for pupils requiring special educational treatment has been sixteen years. This applied in the province even when leaving ages in ordinary schools were lower. During the long period when entry from secondary schools to colleges of further education in the province could take place at fifteen years, pupils attending special schools did not transfer until a year later. However, close relationships between special schools and local further education colleges did evolve in many locations and link courses were a common feature of the special education scene. Many pupils have, however, remained at special schools until they were eighteen. The education authorities have never had specific powers to make special educational provision for young persons over nineteen years nor have such powers been incorporated in the new legislation. Those pupils leaving special schools at eighteen–nineteen who require further specialist treatment are notified to the Health and Social Services Boards for consideration for placement in day care centres or workshops. Pupils attending the special care schools also usually transfer at nineteen to these centres.

One interesting development in the last two years has been the emergence of specialist courses within the Youth Training Programme for school leavers with special needs. This was the Northern Ireland precursor of the Youth Training Scheme in Great Britain. It is funded through DENI by the Northern Ireland Department of Economic Development. Courses for unemployed young persons with special needs have been established on a trial basis in the form of a partnership between a special school and a college of further education, for example the Routeways course on personal and social development for ESN pupils at Downpatrick College. Most of the special schools in the province have also been involved in recent years in Board-sponsored work experience schemes, which have proved particularly effective in assisting special school leavers to select suitable careers and to secure placements. Recently, again through the Youth Training Programme, unemployed special school leavers have attended courses at community workshops run under the auspices of the Department of Economic Development. These have provided specific skills–training in vocational fields relevant to young disabled persons.

The present position

Such then is the current state of the world of special education in Northern Ireland. Like many features of the educational scene in the province it is based on a series of partnerships; between the Education Boards and a variety of voluntary school authorities supported out of public funds; between Education and Health authorities; between central and local government and, most important of all, between parents, teachers and officers with specialist expertise at school level. Nearly 40 years of evolutionary development within this partnership framework have led to the present varied pattern of provision. Currently there are 33 special schools under the overall authority of the Education and Library Boards.

Four of these are schools for physically handicapped children, including one for 'delicate' children – three in Belfast and one in Ballymena; two of the Belfast schools have boarding facilities and serve the whole province. Jordanstown School (maintained, non-denominational status) provides day and boarding facilities for blind and deaf children and for the more severely impaired partially sighted and partially hearing pupils from the whole province. St Francis de Sales School, under Roman Catholic Church voluntary management, caters for deaf children of primary age on a day basis only. Specialist work with secondary age pupils exhibiting severe behavioural problems is undertaken on a residential basis at Fallowfield Boys' School in Craigavon and, on a day basis, at the Jaffe Centre in Belfast.

The remainder of the special schools comprise sixteen schools for children with moderate learning difficulties (ESN) and nine schools attached to hospitals, providing mainly a general education for children hospitalized for long periods. Rosstulla ESN School also has a special unit for children suffering from severe speech defects. Some of the hospital schools have specialist orthopaedic or psychiatric units, where this is a major feature of the on-site medical provision. Of the 24 ESN and hospital schools all but two are controlled schools directly under the management of the Education and Library Boards. These two, one in Belfast and one in Newtownabbey, are Roman Catholic church schools. Only five of the ESN schools retain boarding facilities. This number is likely to decline further as more local special units are set up.

Apart from these separate schools, there are presently 59 special education units attached to controlled or maintained primary and secondary schools throughout the province. These provide specialist facilities for pupils within the catchment areas of a group of schools surrounding the base school. They also allow for a mixture of separate schooling and integration into main school activities, geared to the needs and capabilities of the individual child. Of these units, 25 provide for partially hearing children, 26 for children with severe learning difficulties, two for children with severe speech defects and one for physically handicapped pupils. The remaining six are diagnostic units for the assessment, over an extended period, of children of pre-school and infant school age, prior to a final decision being made regarding placements.

As well as the above schools and units run under the aegis of the Education and Library Boards, there are a further 23 special care schools for severely mentally handicapped children, run by the Health and Social Services Boards. It is these schools which will transfer to the Education and Library Boards in 1987. A summary of this provision is given in the tables on pages 160 and 161.

Parents, health visitors and doctors are encouraged to seek information on special education provision, in the first instance, from the educational psychology department of the appropriate Education and Library Board. Children needing assessment are also referred to these departments by medical staff or, indeed, by headteachers of schools following discussions with the parents concerned. The service is at a major threshold at the present time. The changes which will come in the next two years, although fundamental in a structural and strategic sense, will reflect in many ways slow movements which have already been taking place in the schools, units and classes over several years. Certainly within these institutions and within the teaching, psychological and para-medical professions the foundation stones of a new type of service for

Special Education Provision in Northern Ireland – Summary

Area Board	Type of Establishment	Category of Pupil	Total No.	Cont	Maint	Day	D & R	Board	Prim	Sec	All through
Belfast	Special Schools	Physically handicapped	2	2	0	0	2	0	0	0	2
		Delicate	1	1	0	1	0	0	0	0	1
		Educationally Sub-normal	4	3	1	4	0	0	2	1	1
		Maladjusted	1	1	0	1	0	0	0	1	0
		Deaf	1	0	1	1	0	0	1	0	0
	Special Unit attached to special schools	Diagnostic	1	1	0	1	0	0	1	0	0
	Special units attached to 'ordinary' schools	Partially hearing	5	2	3	5	0	0	2	3	0
		Educationally Sub-Normal	2	0	2	2	0	0	2	0	0
	Hospital schools	Orthopaedic	2	2	0	—	—	0	0	0	2
North Eastern ELB	Special Schools	Physically handicapped	1	1	0	1	0	0	1	0	0
		Educationally Sub-Normal	3	2	1	1	2	0	0	0	3
		Blind and Deaf	1	0	1	0	1	0	0	0	1
	Special units attached to 'ordinary' schools	Partially hearing	5	5	0	5	0	0	2	3	0
		Educationally Sub-Normal	6	6	0	6	0	0	4	2	0
		Diagnostic	2	2	0	2	0	0	2	0	0
South Eastern ELB	Special Schools	Educationally Sub-Normal	5	5	0	3	2	0	1	2	2
	Special units attached to special schools	Diagnostic	1	1	0	1	0	0	1	0	0
	Special units attached 'ordinary' schools	Partially hearing	7	5	2	7	0	0	3	4	0
		Educationally Sub-Normal	5	3	2	5	0	0	5	0	0
		Diagnostic	1	1	0	1	0	0	1	0	0
	Hospital Schools	General illness	1	1	0	—	—	—	0	0	0
		Delicate and psychiatric	1	1	0	—	—	—	0	0	1

Key: Cont – Controlled Maint – Maintained D & R – Day & Residential Board – Boarding Prim – Primary Sec – Secondary

Special Education Provision in Northern Ireland – Summary

Area Board	Type of Establishment	Category of Pupil	Total No.	No. of establishments within the categories shown							
				Cont	Maint	Day	D & R	Board	Prim	Sec	All through
Southern ELB	Special Schools	Maladjusted	1	1	0	0	0	0	1	0	
	Special units attached to 'ordinary' schools	Partially hearing	3	3	0	3	0	0	3	0	0
		Educationally Sub-Normal	12	9	3	12	0	0	7	5	0
		Speech defect	1	0	1	1	0	0	1	0	0
		Physically handicapped	1	0	1	1	0	0	1	0	0
		Diagnostic	2	2	0	2	0	0	2	0	0
	Hospital Schools	General illnesses	3	3	0	—	—	—	—	—	3
Western ELB	Special Schools	Educationally Sub-Normal	4	4	0	2	2	0	0	0	4
	Special units attached to 'ordinary' schools	Partially hearing	5	2	3	5	0	0	4	1	0
		Educationally Sub-Normal	1	1	0	1	0	0	1	0	0
		Speech defects	1	1	0	1	0	0	1	0	0
	Hospital Schools	General illnesses	2	2	0	—	—	—	0	0	2
TOTALS			94	73	21	75 (Hosp Schs not inc)	9	1	48	23	23
Eastern H & SSB	Special care schools	Severe mental handicap	8	—	—	—	—	—	0	0	9
Northern H & SSB	Special care schools	Severe mental handicap	5	—	—	—	—	—	0	0	5
Southern H & SSB	Severe mental handicap	5	—	—	—	—	0	—	0	5	
Western H & SSB	Special care schools	Severe mental handicap	5	—	—	—	—	—	0	0	23
TOTALS			23	—	—	—	—	—	0	0	23

Key: Cont – Controlled   Maint – Maintained   D & R – Day & Residential   Board – Boarding   Prim – Primary   Sec – Secondary children with special educational needs have been laid. To build on these we will need to extend the effective local partnerships to district and area level and to secure and apply the resources necessary for expansion. The next few years should be very interesting and challenging times for all who work in the field of special education in the province.

Special education in Scotland

Special Education in Scotland has a long and worthy history. Schools for the deaf and the blind, established initially by voluntary bodies, have existed for over 160 years, and, since the beginning of the century, the State has been concerned with handicapped children. Up to 1939, much of the legislation was permissive, and provision was uneven throughout the country.

The provisions of the 1946 Education (Scotland) Act, in which the term 'special educational treatment' first occurs, laid a duty on eduction authorities to provide treatment for handicapped pupils as part of the general duty to provide education for all children. In 1947 the Advisory Council on Education was asked to review the provision, and between 1950 and 1952 seven reports were published, each dealing with a specific handicap. In 1954 Special Educational Treatment (Scotland) Regulations were issued, and following this, from 1960 onwards, a number of working parties set up by the Secretary of State issued guidance on ascertainment. A consolidating Act in 1962 was amended by an Act in 1969 which gave power to ascertain children under the age of five. This replaced a power to act only at the parents' request. There was a new emphasis on there being a proper consideration of a number of factors in ascertainment.

Following on the issue of a Report (The Melville Report) an important Act was passed in 1974 – the Education (Mentally Handicapped Children) (Scotland) Act. This discontinued the ascertainment of children as unsuitable for education in school, and imposed a duty to provide for their education whether accommodated in a hospital or otherwise. This meant that Junior Occupation Centres were to be discontinued, become schools and be appropriately staffed with qualified teachers.

The Education (Scotland) Act 1981 has brought the legal position up to date. As with the rest of the UK, the findings of the Warnock

Committee laid the basis for legislation, but a highly important Report – *The Eduction of Pupils with Learning Difficulties in Primary and Secondary Schools* by HMI – issued in 1978, was a second base. In Scotland there has been introduced, through the 1981 Act, legislation to reflect a single fundamental concept of special educational need. This comprehends children who were in special schools/classes or receiving remedial education, and, importantly, also children with learning or other difficulties whose needs hitherto lacked specific recognition. The educational significance is that the influence of the curriculum, teaching methods and organization in creating difficulties are highlighted.

Statutory categories of handicap have been replaced by assessment and recording on the basis of a profile of needs. Much of the legislation is similar to that introduced in England and Wales. The following paragraphs provide details of differences in provision from elsewhere in the UK relating to special educational needs.

The approach to special educational needs

The definition of special educational needs is common to both Acts and is thus intended to identify similar populations. The English Act, (which applies also to Wales), however, assigns to schools a specific role in identifying and meeting the less severe special educational needs (such as those of children receiving remedial education) and in referring the more severe to the LEA. This has no Scottish counterpart. The reasons are structural: English legislation is framed in terms of the provision of schools by LEAs; Scottish legislation prescribes the provision of education. The difference is, however, only between an implicit and an explicit duty.

Children and young persons

The Scottish Act is written in terms of 'children and young persons receiving school education' while the English Act refers only to 'children' but they cover broadly the same school population. Section 135(1) of the Education (Scotland) Act 1980 defines 'child' as a person who is not over school age and 'young person' as a person over school age who has not attained the age of eighteeen years. The English Act defines 'child' as any pupil who has not attained the age of nineteen years. The Scottish legislation includes the distinctive refinement that its provisions in respect of young persons are enabling rather than prescriptive. Handicapped young persons are wherever possible to act on their own behalf; education authorities have a power but not a duty to record them and may not do so without their agreement. The English provisions for under and over-sixteens are not differentiated.

Pre-school children

The provisions for the assessment and recording (or making a statement of) very young children are broadly similar in both Acts, with the important exception that the English Act assigns to authorities a duty to provide for the special educational needs of children who have reached the age of two, while in Scotland the duty applies when children are of school age but a corresponding power exists in respect of all under-fives. This reflects the fact that nursery education in England but not in Scotland has a lower age limit of two years.

Records/statements

Both Acts require specific documentation for children with severe and continuing needs. The Scottish Act uses the term 'record' while the English equivalent is 'statement'. This is essentially a matter of drafting preference: 'record' was the term employed in the Warnock Report. The Secretary of State for Education and Science, during the Second Reading debate of the English Bill, commented that 'because of the variety of connotations of the words "children with records" and matters of that nature . . . it would be unwise to use the word "Record" or "recorded".' No representations on the subject were made in Scotland. However, the shorthand term 'recorded children' appeared acceptable and it avoided a number of drafting difficulties inherent in the English term.

Appeal against decision not to make a statement

The English Act provides that such a decision by a LEA may be subject to appeal to the Secretary of State. No corresponding provision (against a decision not to record) has been included in the

Scottish Act on the grounds that a successful appeal imposing a requirement of the education authority to record would carry with it an implicit requirement to make the necessary provision available. This might be seen as infringing the prerogative of authorities in deploying resources and placing an additional financial burden on them at a time of economic restraint. The English provision was seen as essential because the right in effect already existed. The Secretary of State may take action under section 68 of the Education Act 1944 in circumstances where he is satisfied that the LEA is acting unreasonably. There is no equivalent provision in Scottish educational legislation, action by the Secretary of State being possible only where an authority is in default.

Appeals to local Appeal Committees

The Scottish Act provides for appeals on the school placement of recorded children or young persons to be determined initially by an Appeal Committee, with the possibility of a further appeal to the Sheriff. Similarly referable are decisions by an authority to record, and matters relating to the summary of impairments and the statement of special educational needs contained in the record. The Appeal Committee will be required to refer any professional issues to the Secretary of State for final decision before dealing with that part of a reference relating to a school placing request. The English Act provides for appeals against the special educational provision specified in a statement to be made initially to an appeal committee who will be empowered either to confirm the provision or to refer the case back to the authority with their

Subject of Appeal	Scotland Decision rests with:	England and Wales Decision rests with:

School placement	1 Appeal Committee
	
	2 Sheriff, on parent's
	   appeal
		1 LEA on appeal
		   committee referral
		
		2 Secretary of State

Impairments)
)
)
Statement of needs)
	Secretary of State	1 LEA on appeal
		   committee referral
		
		2 Secretary of State

Resources	–	1 LEA on appeal committee referral 2 Secretary of State

observations for reconsideration, with a further right of appeal to the Secretary of State.

As the table on page 165 shows, the differences in the two Acts relate more to machinery than to the rights thereby given to parents. A difference of principle exists, however, in relation to the right available to a parent in terms of the English Act to question the provision of resources by a LEA.

Appeals against the provision proposed to meet special educational needs were excluded from the Scottish provision on the grounds that such appeals would constitute an additional demand for resources, justified in principle and difficult to refute; and that the allocation of available resources was a matter within the prerogative of the local authority.

Integration and curriculum

The provisions in the English Act regarding integration have no equivalent in Scottish legislation. There have not been in Scotland the same pressures towards integration, though this is in no way precluded by existing statute, and in a number of regions in Scotland there has been considerable development in moving children into mainstream provision. With regard to advice, development and research on curriculum, the Consultative Committee on the Curriculum, the Secretary of State's principal advisory body, has made a priority of the curricular needs and a Committee on Special Educational Needs (COSPEN) chaired by a Deputy Director of Education, has recently successfully completed a three year remit. In the research field, an adequate framework exists for supporting projects. In the Scottish context, the following have been of great interest – the development of multi-disciplinary assessment, the delivery of services in remote areas, the role and functions of the home visiting teachers, and the effectiveness of preparation for adulthood. The following is a brief summary of developments in Scotland affecting provision for Recorded Pupils.

The education of pupils of secondary age with mild mental handicap

An informal national coordinating committee established by HMI has been encouraged by the response to its strategy for curriculum development. The work in 40 pilot schools is well under way. Every region and island authority is participating, and local steering groups chaired by a coordinator oversee the initiatives. Most curricular areas are covered. A noticeable feature is the general enthusiasm with which the initiatives have been pursued and the staff in the pilot schools have demonstrated a capacity for curriculum development which has hitherto been untapped. Support has been readily forthcoming from the advisory service, the child guidance service and colleges of education. There is little doubt that these cooperative ventures have revitalized the curriculum in several pilot schools. All local coordinators have provided interim reports. These have been distributed to all the Regions and Island Authorities so that coordinators are aware of developments in the rest of the country. The national coordinating committee has prepared a note of guidance for the final reports which are due to be completed in June 1985 and will be disseminating the outcomes of these initiatives through seminars and the preparation of a report consisting of two parts: summaries of the work in each school and an examination of relevant issues.

Other curricular initiatives

Schools for pupils with mild mental handicap are also taking account of developments in mainstream education, in particular the introduction of Standard Grade examinations. The retention in special schools of an increasing number of young persons beyond the age of sixteen has made course development for sixteen to eighteens as relevant to these schools as to mainstream secondary schools and further education colleges. Some of the modules which have been developed for mainstream are applicable, with modification, in special schools but other access modules will have to be devised in order to bring young persons in special schools up to the level of the Action Plan modules.

The Inspectorate PYPAD Report and Seminar (*Provision for Young People and Adults with Severe, Complex and Long-Term Disabilities*) highlighted the role community education services could play in helping the handicapped in the community.

The publication of *Learning together* by COSPEN has brought a much needed boost to the curriculum in schools for pupils with severe mental handicap. There has been a follow up to the publication by members of the subcommittee in each education authority and in most colleges of education, and education authorities themselves are now considering strategies for supporting the developments.

There are, of course, the other successful enterprises by COSPEN: publication on good practice in mathematics, language arts, and environmental studies; cooperation with the Scottish Health Education Group; the Curriculum Development Materials document; and the micro-electronic enterprises.

Education in mental handicap hospitals

The progress report by HM Inspectors of Schools, prepared in collaboration with colleagues from SSHD and Central Advisory Service of SWSG, was published in March 1984. A follow-up conference with education officers and staff from colleges of education took place in August 1984.

Education (Scotland) Act 1981

Both parents and professionals have commented favourably on the level and quality of parental involvement. There has been widespread praise for the Future Needs Assessment. There is not, as yet, any firm evidence of the number of recorded pupils in mainstream schools.

Microtechnology and special educational needs

The three regional development centre schools have been provided with a wide range of equipment. Staff have become acquainted with both hardware and software, and centres are taking on the wider role of assisting other schools. The Special Educational Needs Information Exchange Project has made significant progress. It has great potential for curriculum development. The database has been established at SCET and modems have been placed in all the participating schools and colleges.

All schools for pupils with mild mental handicap have or will receive a micro-special pack consisting of a video, a magazine and over twenty pieces of software. The software is being produced by the Scottish Microelectronics Development Programme (SMDP) with the cooperation of groups of teachers largely from Scottish special schools. The magazine contains a large number of articles on the use of computers in special schools written by Scottish contributors, and a video which contains examples of good practice in the use of computers.

Educational psychologists

The new legislation makes heavy demands on the educational psychologists. A number of authorities have taken steps to provide additional posts to meet increased workloads arising from better preschool and post-sixteen provision and the new assessment procedures associated with the Record of Needs. The training and recruitment of educational psychologists has been the subject of much discussion and consultation and proposals for change are presently before the Convention of Local Authorities and the Scottish Education Department.

Teacher training

The training of teachers is, as elsewhere, of great importance. In Scotland the General Teaching Council has no category of registration for teachers in special education. Teachers who wish to work in this field have in the first place to obtain registration as a primary or secondary teacher. A significant development in the opportunities for qualification is the establishment of a diploma (in learning difficulties) for teachers in mainstream schools who now work as learning support teachers and this is a high grade qualification. Serving teachers selected are seconded on either a full or part-time basis to study for the diploma.

Under the Special Aid Scheme, 60 teachers enrolled in courses commencing in April 1984. The three qualification courses at Moray House, Jordanhill and St Andrew's Colleges of Education have now been validated by CNAA.

An ad hoc committee continues to meet to keep developments in teacher training for special educational needs (recorded pupils) under review. One of the important initiatives is the establishment of a group of tutors for courses for teachers of pupils with severe and profound mental handicap to explore their deployment as a national resource in the colleges.

Education of the deaf

Fieldwork has been completed for the survey by HMI on the education of hearing-impaired children. The draft report will probably be completed by the end of June 1985. The report will not be in the book-stalls but will be circulated widely.

Research

This includes the following projects:

1. Identifying and meeting the needs of profoundly mentally handicapped children. This research by Jordanhill College of Education has proved valuable and contributed greatly to developments in this area of complex special educational needs.

2. Transition from school to further education. This work has been published by the Scottish Council for Research in Education and is based on interesting practice in local authorities.

3. A study of provision made in local authorities for visually impaired pupils – due for completion in summer 1985.

4. Meeting the special educational needs of the mentally handicapped. This is a research project started in 1985 to look at the working of the 1981 legislation in terms of the provision made by education authorities.

All those concerned with education, health and social work services for children and young people have a major task in developing the services on the lines recommended and much progress has been made.

Special education in Wales

The development of special education in Wales has been broadly along the same lines as in England. The same legal framework applies in Wales as in England. The eight shire counties are the local education authorities, with identical powers and duties as their English counterparts. Successive measures of administrative devolution – primary and secondary education in 1970 and further and higher education in 1978 – have not affected this framework. The differences have been mainly matters of relationships, arising from closer contact between the Welsh Office and the local authorities, and also from a sensitive understanding by the Welsh Office of local conditions, where, for example, differences in tradition, outlook and culture have affected the nature or ethos of the service.

Special educational provision has accordingly assumed the usual pattern, with special schools and units concentrated mainly in the more populous areas of the south and north. In the sparsely populated rural areas, which comprise the major part of Wales, the usual difficulties have been encountered of making provision for tiny minorities, widely dispersed geographically, and authorities facing such problems have had of necessity to make some use of out-county provisions. In recent years, however, and in anticipation of the Warnock recommendations, there has been a growing trend for authorities to make their own provision, relying on out-county places only for the less common and mutliple handicaps. As in England, efforts to reduce segregation of handicapped pupils have been given added impetus by considerations of finance. The requirements of the Education Act 1981 have thus accentuated a trend which was already gathering momentum – a trend which has had implications also for those authorities which customarily provided for the out-county needs, since the loss of out-county pupils has necessitated a review of possible over-provision of special school places.

There is, however, an important and distinctive dimension in Wales, which has had substantial educational, organizational and financial consequences – the Welsh language which in regard to special educational needs involves making provision for a minority of a minority. This affects not only the Welsh language strongholds of Gwynedd and Dyfed but also the highly anglicized counties of the south and the north-east, where there has been spectacular growth in recent years of schools, primary and secondary, which use Welsh as the main medium of instruction.

This interesting phenomenon has not been without its problems, not the least of which has been the provision of adequate supplies of teaching materials. The production of Welsh language textbooks, for example, is not commercially feasible because of low demand. The Welsh local education authorities, in recognition of this fact, have made brave attempts to solve the problem by acting cooperatively through the agency of the Welsh Joint Education Committee, which for many years now has produced a steady but still inadequate supply of textbooks and general readers for Welsh-medium schools. A major advance, however, was made following the 1980 Education Act, which under Section 21 empowered central government to give specific grants to Welsh language education. The WJEC as a result has a greatly enhanced programme, and the prospect of Welsh language schools is considerably brighter.

As usual, of course, public examination candidates continue inexorably to merit priority. But there is a glimmer of light for Welsh speakers with learning difficulties in that the WJEC is committed to the publication of assessment and teaching materials produced specifically for them by the former Committee for Wales of the Schools Council.

Much more, however, remains to be done if the complex problem is to be satisfactorily solved. The complexity is compounded by population sparsity and the categories of educational need are many: slow learners for whom a bilingual education may impose particular stresses and who in the ordinary school may need extra care and teaching; pupils whose needs cannot adequately be met in the ordinary school and who may require a special school or unit where the teaching medium is Welsh; the severely or multiply handicapped, for whom a residential place is essential and who have in consequence to be boarded in an anglicized environment or even cross into England. Cases such as these, where a child's sole linguistic experience is within a Welsh-speaking family present an acute dilemma of a choice between suitable educational provision and the serious consequences of isolation from the family, the removal of community support and exposure to an unfamiliar language.

With the combined effects of the requirements of the 1981 Act and of parental pressures, the tendency is increasingly for such children to be accommodated in the ordinary school with as much extra support by way of staff and equipment as possible. Gwynedd, for example, is now dealing in this way both with sight and with hearing handicaps. But the extra needs faced by authorities with bilingual communities are considerable, both in terms of financial resources and of extra manpower and equipment. There is indeed a continuing need for suitably qualified staff who are Welsh-speaking and qualified for work amongst pupils with special educational needs – not only teachers, but staff from other disciplines, such as psychologists, medical and paramedical staff and social workers.

Thus the common statutory basis shared by Welsh and English authorities is not the whole of the story. In many respects Welsh authorities have the same problems as their English counterparts; but there is the added factor of the language, which in regard to special educational needs especially, demands not merely resources, dedication and skills, but sympathy and understanding for those children who, although few in number, might all too easily be overlooked.

11 An international perspective

The limitations of the perspective

This chapter is not an attempt to summarize educational responses to those with special educational needs on a worldwide basis. Such a task would be impossible in a book of this length, let alone a single chapter, without resorting to statements of such a generalized and superficial nature as to be of little practical value, if not entirely meaningless. So the aim is to highlight those recent developments in other countries which seem to be most relevant to our immediate post-Warnock position in the UK. Almost inevitably examples are drawn from the so-called developed nations rather than the developing ones; not that it is by any means the case that the wealthiest societies necessarily respond to the needs of the handicapped more sensitively, or more imaginatively, than the less well off. But the rich nations do have two networks for their almost exclusive use through which they can broadcast their own achievements and draw upon the good practice of others. One is the European Economic Community, the other the Organization of Economic Cooperation and Development. The membership of the former is well-known – the 'Ten' – now to be extended to 'Twelve' to include Spain and Portugal, both of which countries have a keen interest in extending educational opportunity for the handicapped and a firm commitment to integrative practices. The membership of OECD embraces the countries of Western Europe, thus overlapping the EEC, North America, Australia and Japan with Yugoslavia in affiliation; in other words an association of the relatively successful capitalist nations, created out of enlightened self-interest. Through its Centre for Educational Research and Innovation it has since 1976 managed a far-reaching project concerned with the education of the handicapped adolescent, generously funded by successive United States administrations with a continuing commitment until at least the end of 1986.

The EEC has also sponsored work in this area, initially as a contribution to the International Year of the Disabled in 1981. Three themes have been identified:

1. vocational and occupational training;
2. the education of children;
3. technical aids for the disabled.

Such a broad base can clearly cover anything a member country wishes to include and indeed progress has been hampered by difficulties of interpretation. The OECD, whilst not defining precisely what it chooses to mean either by the words 'handicapped' or 'adolescent', nevertheless from the outset decided to exclude from consideration disabilities caused by social or economic deprivation and identified as the two key areas 'Integration'[1] and 'Transition from school to working life'.[2] Both projects have significantly raised the level of awareness, not only on the part of member governments but also of professional workers, in relation to the nature of handicap. The OECD work in particular has also been successful in forging links between educators in member countries, particularly those responsible for the administration of special needs programmes. For example, a number of education officers with a special education brief in LEAs have visited those with similar responsibilities in the USA and have received reciprocal visits, leading to a good understanding of each other's working methods.

Thus as a result of these two projects special educators in the UK now have a much more ready access to information in other developed countries; this of itself may well have distracted attention from the developing world as well as the Eastern Bloc, from both of which there is no doubt much to learn as well as to teach.

Common issues – differing responses

The EEC estimates that the Community's handicapped population is at least 27 million. Immediately this presents a key issue – how is the group requiring special educational treatment to be defined? There is a widespread appreciation in most countries, certainly of Western Europe and North America, perhaps less so in Australasia, that it is often society which handicaps the individual – by not providing ramps to buildings, for example, rather than the nature of an individual disability. But more crucial is the severity of the disability – are those who learn to read slowly to be included? Those with mild hearing loss in part of the register? Those who find it difficult to conform to the mores of a so-called 'normal' school? And so on.

There is no agreement. In the USA, approximately nine per cent of the population are affected by the keynote legislation under which education for the handicapped must be provided – Federal Law 94·142. The Scandinavian countries have difficulty in identifying any proportion at all because of their fervent commitment to integration at all stages of education and within society at large. In Australia a significant number of children are excluded from access to education as a result of medical examination.

So the size and nature of the client group are variable; but so are the means by which individuals are identified as in need of special educational treatment. Whilst it is generally appreciated, at least by those delivering services to the handicapped, that handicap is no longer an intrinsic and unmodifiable flaw, in most countries it is recognized that before a disability can be overcome it must be identified precisely; this practical need often clashes with the desire to avoid labelling. In the Scandinavian countries the latter prevails; by contrast with Australia and New Zealand, medical examinations produce a precise categorization for many handicapped children, some of whom are thereby excluded from educational services altogether.

The most dominant issue in recent years, and one common to all developed countries, has been that of integration, both within mainstream schooling and within society at large. Interpretations vary as does the degree of commitment to thorough-going policies, but the international movement of opinion and of practice has been in the same direction.

Less universal is the attitude to providing access to paid employment for the handicapped. The Norwegians believe such opportunity to be a fundamental right, in spite of the experience which they share of dramatically increasing levels of unemployment. Others, including many in the USA, are looking increasingly for alternatives – 'significant living without work' as the late Jack Tizzard[3] termed it in a seminal paper.

There is considerable variation too in the extent to which work preparation is generally – 'educationally orientated' – or specific training geared to fitting the disabled young person to perform a defined task in a particular work place. The effectiveness of parental pressure and that of advocacy groups for the handicapped is variable but in most countries such pressure is becoming a more potent factor both on government policy and in relation to the level of services provided for individuals. In the USA it is now relatively common for local school boards either to be threatened with, or be actually taken to the courts, in order to secure what the parent sees to be appropriate educational provision.

Identification and assessment

We have already seen that the widely-shared dilemma can be summed up as how to identify needs effectively without also reaping the counter-productive aspects of labelling. It has long been recognized, particularly in the United States, that labelling can actually reinforce handicap[4]; a blind rehabilitation programme for the partially-sighted often leads to the acquisition of the attitudes and behaviour patterns of the blind as described by R A Scott in *The Making of the Blind Man.*[5] A disproportionate number of young people from ethnic minority groups have found themselves categorized as mentally retarded; whether Puerto Ricans in the USA, Maoris in New Zealand or the children of Turkish immigrants in West Germany. The net effect is often to limit the educational and social opportunities rather than to enhance them[6].

So the dangers are well understood but so too is the crucial importance of identifying disabilities as early as possible, and traditionally in many countries a dozen or so categories broadly parallel to those used in the UK prior to Warnock have been used – mentally retarded, blind or partially sighted, orthopaedically handicapped and so on. Increasingly such stark labelling is abandoned in favour of preparing a prescription based on identified needs. In the USA the specific labels are now more commonly embraced within such categories as learning or developmentally disabled; but it is then necessary to make the prescription precise, if appropriate educational, psychological and medical services are to be provided. Professor Nicholas Hobbs and colleagues at Vanderbilt University, Tennessee, have made a trenchant criticism of traditional models of assessing handicap:

> Classical categories obscure individual differences.
>
> There is an assumption that the problem is exclusive to the individual.
>
> An individual is normally only 'assigned' to one category whereas handicapped people frequently have secondary handicap.

Classifications are 'deficit oriented' and do not recognize strengths or 'ecological assets'.

Classical categories tend to be static and take no account of a changed environment.

In order to overcome these deficiencies Hobbs has proposed what he calls 'an ecologically orientated service-based classification system'[2] which has been influential both in the USA and elsewhere in changing practice. The system's main features are:

Classification is on the basis of services required to achieve specified goals during a particular period of life.

The 'ecological assessment' aims to improve the 'fit' between the individual and the important people and places in his life.

Services are specified to enable the individual to function in his environment at a given time – not to 'make him perfect'.

Modifications will almost certainly be necessary to other people and places as well as the handicapped individual.

The 'enablement plan' must spell out action to be taken and by whom.

A multi-disciplinary assessment conference produces a schedule of things to be done.

This model is neither unique nor revolutionary and looks very like a description of best practice in many countries, including the UK.

But the influence of Hobbs' work, which was originally undertaken in relation to handicapped adolescents, is now widespread throughout the countries of the OECD as a result of his early participation in the project.

Whilst it could not be claimed that any country can yet identify all substantial disabilities pre-school and define needs precisely, there has undoubtedly been a marked improvement within the last decade both in countries like Sweden with a high level of established provision and Spain or Portugal where development has been much more recent. In this, as in other respects, trans-national dissemination of both theory and practice has been influential.

Integration in schools

If faced with the question 'Do you integrate handicapped pupils in your country?' almost any special educator is likely to answer 'Yes . . ., but . . .' Perhaps the Italians are able to answer 'Yes' with least equivocation. No half measures are allowed philosophically.

Various Acts passed by the national parliament in the 1970s amount to 'an invitation to join the normal conditions of life'. A clear distinction is drawn between education taking place within regular classes of the public schools and all other forms of provision, and only the former can legally be called 'integration'. All children have the right to an integrated education so defined. Most Italian teachers and parents would regard anything else as a denial of a basic human right. The *standards* of provision, however, the extra facilities, specialist staff and curriculum and so on, may well be less satisfactory in Italy than in countries such as France with a less purist definition of integration.

Generally, though, classes are small, with a maximum of twenty, the *bidelli*, school helpers who have both cleaning and pastoral responsibilities, often make a particular contribution to caring for handicapped pupils. The atmosphere in Italian schools is generally free and relaxed, with teachers tolerant to fairly high noise levels. Formal assessment of pupils according to a ten point scale has been abandoned in favour of *giudizi* – informal judgements or profiles. A high priority is given to socialization and to the nature of the adult-child relationships. Support teachers are assigned to classrooms to work alongside the regular teachers and not specifically with handicapped pupils. However, some provincial authorities, for example the City of Rome, have attempted to organize withdrawal groups but frequently have to back down when faced with the rooted opposition of the teachers' unions. The most severely handicapped may have the exclusive help of a full-time assistant sitting beside them in the regular class.

All schools are guaranteed by law the support of a team consisting of a social worker, an educational psychologist and a physiotherapist. However, not surprisingly, the reality is, as in other countries, that such specialist support is often inadequate to meet all demands, or for some schools non-existent. Again unsurprisingly, integration appears to be more capable of achievement at the elementary level; the secondary schools experience substantial problems in providing curricula which are appropriate for those with learning difficulties, for the pupils of middling ability and also stretching the brightest – even where the staff are totally committed to integration. On the other hand there is evidence that the attitude of Italian society generally to the adult disabled is considerably more knowledgeable and understanding than that encountered elsewhere.

Most countries in recent years have experienced growing pressure to integrate schools as only one of a number of pressures. Potentially the most difficult to accommodate alongside a policy of integration has been that to raise standards of achievement generally and to make the curriculum for the majority more 'relevant'. The balance of priority between the handicapped and non-handicapped has frequently seemed difficult to achieve. In the USA, for example, nearly one in five pupils are entitled under the Federal Law 94·142 to a statement of special need and to have appropriate educational and other services delivered to them – including a prescription for individualized learning. Apart from the inevitable encouragement to parents to resort to the courts to gain their legal rights, as mentioned earlier, this process has also stimulated a demand on the part of parents of non-handicapped children for an individualized programme and for an equivalent amount of attention to be paid to the particular needs, educational and other, of their children. The concerns expressed in the Federal Government-backed publication *A Nation at Risk* in 1984 have tended to elevate the quest for higher standards above that for integration.

Yet one area of the USA in particular has become renowned world-wide for the success of its integration policy in the public schools system – Madison, Wisconsin. Two special educators, Lee Grunwald and Jerry Schroeder, decided to make a reality of their belief that all pupils and students should be educated in the 'least restrictive environment'. They identified a small number of schools in their district which could be modifed to provide a barrier-free environment. Within these schools the educational programme is seen as an entity with the Principal responsible for all aspects, thus avoiding the creation of a parallel special education programme – and chain of command – where special units are added to regular schools. The involvement of community organizations, particularly with the most severely handicapped, is seen as crucial not only in providing scarce support to the teachers but also as part of the process of modifying community attitudes and preparing the way for the handicapped young person to take his place in society.

The considerable achievements of the Madison programme clearly rest not only on the foresight and commitment of the educational administrators, as well as the development of specific functional curricula for the handicapped, but also a carefully planned and coordinated investment – of teacher training and preparation, peripatetic specialist teachers, ancilliaries, therapists and diagnostic and evaluation services.

It is not only every country that starts from where its traditions have brought it in terms of integration, but also localities within countries. Certainly within the USA it would not be difficult to identify areas as far at the end of the spectrum from Madison as could be found in those countries where the belief in separate provision is firmly retained.

Not that the reality across countries – or within countries – is at all well delineated. Sweden has many times stated official policy as being integration; yet often children are educated entirely in separate units on the regular school campus, or even in separate establishments altogether. France has declared the *loi d'orientation en faveur des personnes handicappés*, whereby priority is given to solutions which place the handicapped pupil in the natural enviroment; but the gap between legislation and practice has yet to be substantially bridged. In Norway ordinary schools cannot refuse to admit the handicapped if parents insist. Nevertheless separate provision still exists and special 'support centres' for the handicapped have recently been created. The severely and multiply handicapped are entirely excluded from New Zealand's educational system.

The halting and uneven progress towards integration should not be seen as springing from a lack of regard on the part of educators and other professionals for the needs of the young handicapped, but rather as an expression of the genuine dilemma as to whether total integration really does always enhance the educational opportunities of individuals. No doubt too there are governments whose educational priorities are not always headed by the needs of the handicapped. What is inevitably the case is that examples of good practice can be found where integration is total on the Italian model, where special classes or units have been created, where the handicapped are integrated for part of the curriculum and withdrawn for others and, very widely, in special schools.

The curriculum

'It is those forms of organization which are prepared to allow for individual rates of learning which ultimately achieve the best and most consistent results'.[7] We have seen that individualized learning programmes are now supported by Federal Law in the USA. In many other countries too their importance is generally recognized. Whilst the Norwegians are fairly committed to a mainstreaming policy, they are equally determined to differentiate both in terms of curricular content and specialist teaching skills in order to meet the particular needs of the handicapped. A team teaching approach is therefore common. Whilst the French system is still, mostly, a segregated one, teaching style, and therefore the delivery of the curriculum, have changed markedly in recent years. It is widely recognized that teacher intervention is an aid to learning, not its cause and that it is for the school to ensure that its practices and objectives do not impose additional handicaps – for example, an over concentration on the narrow enhancement of academic standards at the expense of curricular breadth and social objectives.

Parallel to enhanced emphasis on individual needs has been the move to a more vocationally-orientated curriculum even for those under the age of sixteen. In the last 30 years in France, 80 *Ecoles Nationales de Perfectionnement* have been established catering for youngsters between the age of twelve and seventeen who are mildly retarded (Wechsler 65–80). The curriculum offered at one such school in the Orne is fairly typical; for the first two years all receive a basic education for 26 hours a week with a heavy concentration on Maths and French. Thereafter there is an emphasis on developing communication skills and relating classroom study to practical activities. A vocational training programme now occupies between 50 per cent and 60 per cent of the pupils' time, each concentrating on one of four areas – horticulture, building, carpentry and painting/decorating/glazing. Much work is commissioned from outside the school and the 'going rate' often paid. Pupils frequently travel to employers' premises and towards the end of their school career are found work placements of between one and three months.

This pattern prompts two considerations which are of increasing concern in many countries. The first is the extent to which vocational orientation should be specific, particularly during the school years. Many American and Australian special educators believe that the more specific and task-related the training the greater the opportunity for paid employment once the youngster leaves full-time education, and there is much evidence to support this view. The work of Mark Gold and Tom Bellamy in the USA has demonstrated that severely mentally handicapped young people can become employable provided the training is related to the nature of their disability. Mark Gold's principle 'let's try another way' has become something of a catch-phrase in this respect. On the other hand, many express concern in 'programming' a mildly handicapped young person at as early a stage as thirteen years of age to become, for example, a building worker.

The second consideration is related and concerns the establishment of repetitive curricula. Unless those responsible for educational programmes coordinate their activities at each stage of the young person's development, it is possible, indeed likely – given the universal preoccupation with vocational preparation and enhancement of social and communication skills, – that he or she will be presented with very similar curricular offerings at both the school and the further education or transitional stage.

The curricular development which has perhaps attracted most attention internationally in recent years has been Instrumental Enrichment[8]. The programme was originally developed in Israel by Professor Reuven Feuerstein[9] and is now well established in schools, both special and mainstream, in USA, Canada, Australasia and the UK. The intention is firstly to explore what children *could* learn as opposed to conventional testing which in general records only what *has been* learned.

The second major element is the recognition that the majority of learners need an interpretation of experience and this process Feuernstein describes as 'mediation'. Thus Instrumental Enrichment rests on the conviction that cognitive skills can be developed and that potential to learn is crucially influenced by the quality of mediation.

The emphasis is on problem solving and thus developing the thinking skills of planning, searching, comparing, and drawing conclusions. The material is relatively 'content free', consisting of pencil and paper tasks, and in effect amounts to a fresh start for pupils who may have a long record of relative failure within the normal learning processes. A key element is the teaching style required. Pupil participation must be ensured and any strategy or solution proposed by the learner has to be discussed. Experiences gained through the task or 'Instrument' need to be constantly related by the teacher to the pupils' general experience – both in the rest of the curriculum and in solving the problems of living. This process is known as 'bridging' and does of course require a high level of sensitivity and skill on the part of the teacher. It is essential, therefore, that teachers are carefully selected and receive intensive training in the use of the materials.

It seems likely that the use of Instrumental Enrichment will become more widespread; already teachers and special educators in Spain, Portugal, Italy and the Scandinavian countries have had experience of it. It is probable too that national versions based on similar principles will be developed. Clearly the integration of such a programme with the rest of the curriculum is a crucial issue, as is the extent to which such programmes are regarded as solely of potential benefit to handicapped pupils.

Transition from school to work

Most developed countries display two potentially conflicting features in recent years – a substantial growth in unemployment levels amongst young people and increased aspirations on the part of many handicapped youngsters, their parents and their teachers. The response to both has usually been an attempt to enhance the employability of the young disabled by work preparation courses, work experience, specialist careers counselling and enlisting the aid of sympathetic potential employers. The elements in such programmes frequently bear a close resemblance to each other in whichever country they might be based.

The *Daniskole* could be seen as a prototype of the new wave of transition projects in Scandinavia. One such was opened in 1970 in an old farmhouse with 25 acres near the sea. The Principal is a former merchant seaman who had trained as a teacher but became disillusioned with the theoretical diet he was expected to offer in ordinary Danish secondary schools – particularly rigid and unsatisfactory for those experiencing difficulty in learning to read and write, 'whose failures were built on failure'. He believed practical skills could be a better way to learning. Practical work is not, however, an end in itself. The students engage in farming, fishing, gardening, cooking and sewing. The metal, glass fibre and wood workshops have a dual purpose, to produce goods for use by the community and also stimulate a desire on the part of the youngsters to acquire academic skills as it becomes obvious to them that they are necessary in order to carry out their tasks. Staff are a mixture of trained teachers and craftsmen and women, helped by local farmers, fishermen and others. Much of the rebuilding and extension of the farmhouse has been undertaken by the students. A coastal trading ship has been purchased with financial help not only of the Government but also the EEC. It operates commercially, carrying grain between ports on the German and Baltic coast, crewed partly by four to six girls and boys with one or two instructors at a time.

All students are members of a working group and the community is largely self-sufficient. A new cabin has been built for the coaster, old vehicles are renovated, clogs are manufactured both for use and sale to visitors. The residential aspect is seen as crucial, 'you can't run back every night and cry,' as one student put it. Young people between fourteen and nineteen come initially for a year and about a third continue for a second year as they are considered not ready to leave. All have substantial specific handicaps such as epilepsy, blindness, autism. Inevitably the proportion who go on to sheltered rather than open employment or to other forms of full-time education and training has increased recently because of the worsening employment situation.

Less radical – and more typical – are the courses established for Australian school-leavers. Work Preparation Centres such as the Granville Centre in Sydney recruit trainees in the fifteen–nineteen age group – up to fifty at any one time. Referral is by schools, parents or guidance services. The majority have mild intellectual handicaps but also a number have slight sensory disabilities and emotional problems. The centre is firmly work and production oriented. The admission process is thorough, involving at least four 'orientation' visits by potential students to the centre, an assessment week involving the key professional workers and final selection by a committee. The course lasts from nine to twelve months, going through stages with each having a fixed target in terms of both production and behaviour. Initially the balance is 40 per cent work, 60 per cent education, finally moving to the achievement of paid open employment. The rehabilitation counsellors keep contact during the first six months of such employment. In 1983, 37 per cent did in fact achieve this objective, while the rest went on to other work therapy or training schemes or were without occupation.

The record of achievement of open employment has inevitably called into question in Australia as elsewhere, whether it remains sensible to assume that the vast majority of the young disabled will progress from school to work. Generally, though, the enhancement of employability remains the key objective.

At an OECD sponsored Seminar in Arizona in 1983 special educators from a number of developed countries gave general assent to the following useful summary in relation to the transitional stage:

Structural unemployment is likely to increase as new technologies develop, but the predominance of the work ethic in western society must not mean that the handicapped are the sole group uniquely to be denied access to paid employment.

The absence of services once the disabled are employed presents the danger of regression and possible loss of employment.

Whilst enforced quota systems may not be the most effective means of achieving employment for the handicapped, large employers, particularly public services, ought to be pressed to produce written employment policies on the principle of equal access.

Mechanistic work preparation courses with specific goals and behavioural objectives result in substantial gain in competences, but personal experiences not amenable to measurement also need to be offered.

Career and vocational education and counselling should not be confined to the latter years of schooling. Perhaps the greatest shared concern is the extreme patchiness of services delivered in different parts of almost every country. It is usually fortuitous, depending upon where the handicapped young person happens to live, whether he has access to a work preparation course, or even careers counselling. The universal dissemination of good practice and funding levels by both central and regional governments are obviously crucial in raising the general standard of provision to that of the best.

Obviously these statements are not comprehensive and mask many differences of emphasis between countries; nevertheless the development of transitional courses and the increased attention given to the world of work in schools are discernible universally.

Messages from abroad

It is probably true that whatever course the special educator in the UK wishes to espouse – integration, behaviourism, separate provision, or whatever – a successful model can be located somewhere. Nevertheless certain messages from abroad are clear and relatively uncontroversial. Few nations now exclude the severely handicapped from the educational process. Most espouse the course of integration, normalization, 'least restrictive environment' – the terminology varies – with enthusiasm. This does not mean that differentiated teaching either in special school, unit or by withdrawal from ordinary classes is disappearing. Indeed, it is the norm, although forms vary considerably. Nor would UK special educators be wise to follow their Italian counterparts without considering that an 'invitation to normal life' issued to the handicapped can also be an invitation to much less satisfactory quality and breadth of service provision than is achieved in our special schools and units. The more thoroughgoing the integration the more likely it is to raise the possibility of resources of all kinds being spread too thinly.

Funding has become an increasingly important issue in many

countries in recent years, as it has in the UK. The experience of many LEAs that the new arrangements for identification, assessment and statementing have necessitated the employment of more administrators, more psychologists, more specialist teachers and so on, had already been anticipated by the experience in the USA following the enactment of Federal Law 94·142. Unless a determinedly unresponsive stance is taken by central and local government, what has already happened – particularly in Scandinavia, North America and Australasia – is likely to occur in the UK; that is, legislation ensuring more effective identification of handicap, leading to the development of educational and other services which then prompts enhanced expectations on behalf of young people and their parents. The growth in influence of advocacy groups is instructive in this respect. Already organizations such as MENCAP can and do exert political influence upon UK governments as well as having leverage at the local level. But they and other groups have a considerable way to go before they can match their counterparts in the USA, for example. Nevertheless their activities as successful parliamentary lobbyists are likely to become equally potent and their role in advising and supporting parents seeking appropriate services from local authorities more widespread. Given the almost inevitable financial restrictions upon the providers, recourse to law is likely to be a frequent occurrence in the future with parents supported by advocacy groups demanding what they see as legal entitlements – now a common phenomenon in many American states.

The curriculum traditionally provided for both mildly and severely handicapped in the UK is more broad-based, 'liberal' and holistic compared with what can often be found in other countries. Whilst our position is entirely defensible in relation to schooling, provided the curriculm introduces pupils to the world of work, we would be well advised to consider the substantial achievements by those in other countries who concentrate on narrowly conceived skill training beyond school, aiming to provide individuals with immediately marketable skills. As unskilled jobs are disappearing universally, it becomes more and more crucial that the handicapped should have something immediately to offer to a potential employer. In the USA particularly the extent to which university teaching staff have been personally involved not only in developing curricular packages but also instructing handicapped adolescents and securing work placements for them is impressive. The work of Bellamy, Schwartz and others at the University of Oregon is a model in this respect. In contrast, UK universities and other higher educational establishments, even some further education colleges, appear to have little or no direct contact with the handicapped population. However skilled a nation's special educators are in enhancing the employability of the handicapped, there is no gainsaying that many will be without paid open employment for much of all of their adult lives. So in the last five years particularly, increasing attention has been given in many countries to the prospect of educating for 'significant living without work'. This may involve a preparation for participation in voluntary activities; for in most societies there is no shortage of work but only of the means to pay for it to be done. Also more attention has been given to communal living projects and mutual suport groups. The additional contribution which adult and continuing education might make is worth considering in the context of other countries' achievements. Yet many will share the concern so deeply held in Norway and Sweden that only when significant living without work becomes acceptable for all should it be assumed to be a fit objective for the disabled.

Perhaps most significant of all is the enhanced attention which has been focussed upon the educational and other needs of the handicapped in recent years. There is no doubt that this has been facilitated by the developing network of contacts across national boundaries. All countries share the challenge of bringing the general standard of provision up to that of current best practice. Such a formidable task is more likely to be achieved if those responsible for delivering services are prepared to draw on expertise, experience and practical example across the world rather than simply within their own boundaries.

References

1. *The Education Of The Handicapped Adolescent – Integration.* Edited by John Fish HMI OECD Paris 1982
2. *The Education Of The Handicapped Adolescent – Transition from School to Working Life.* Edited by Barry Taylor, OECD Paris 1983
3. *Significant Living Without Work*, paper by the late Jack Tizzard and the late Elizabeth Anderson, OECD Paris 1980
4. *Labelling Of The Mentally Retarded*, J R Mercler, University of California 1973
5. *The Making Of The Blind Man*, Russell Sage, New York 1969
6. *The Dynamic Assessment of Retarded Performers*, University Park Press 1979
7. *Etude comparée de 4 types d'organisation a le'école elementaire*, Foucambert, INRP Paris 1979

8. *Making Up Our Minds*. Report of Schools Council Instrumental Enrichment Project, K Weller & A Croft, Schools Council 1983

9. *Instrumental Enrichment*, R Feuerstein, University Park Press, Baltimore 1979

12 Conclusion: future needs and developments

Special education in the 1980s reveals, both among local authorities and different countries, a remarkable similarity of issues. They share common problems and for the most part common convictions as to how they should be tackled, with strategies adapted to meet varying circumstances.

The basic principle is the recognition of the right of all children, irrespective of abilities or disabilities, to receive a full and effective education compatible with their individual needs to prepare them to share in and to contribute to normal life within the community. There is general agreement also that to achieve this involves maximizing opportunities for those with special needs to be educated in the ordinary school, with the addition of such support and help as may be needed, and minimizing the degree of segregation from ordinary life and activities; in other words, aiming at the greatest possible measure of integration compatible with meeting any special needs an individual may have.

Integration itself is capable of many different interpretations, ranging from education in units on the same campus which, while giving opportunities for sharing in the life of the school community, may produce almost as much isolation as education in a separate school, to total integration with special needs being provided for in mainstream classes. The guiding principle must inescapably be what measure of integration, or for that matter separate treatment, is in the best interests of each child. As the Warnock Committee saw very clearly, there will be a continuing need in the foreseeable future for some separate special schools, particularly for children with severe physical, sensory, intellectual and multiple handicaps, severe behavioural and emotional problems, as well as for those who encounter difficulties in coping in a large mainstream school setting. It in effect becomes a judgement to be made in each individual case as to the point at which the benefits of special provision outweigh the disadvantages of segregation. Where special schools do continue, moreover, it will be important that they should do everything possible to combine their advantages with maximum opportunities for close cooperation and involvement with the mainstream of school and community life to minimize and break down any sense of isolation they might otherwise feel.

The Warnock Committee envisaged that working out and implementing their recommendations would take the rest of this century and beyond. Without belittling the achievements of authorities both before and since 1978, the Warnock estimate is a realistic one; indeed, the 1981 Act, while acknowledged to be a significant step forward, had very little to say on the three Warnock top priorities – under fives, post-sixteens and teacher training. With much yet to be accomplished, it is essential to maintain the momentum of interest and progress in special educational needs which in the last decade led to Warnock and which Warnock itself carried forward and accentuated. There are dangers of slackening effort and with competing pressures the temptations to do so are strong. It is all too easy to convince oneself that a few modest adjustments to what already exists are all that are needed – a few handicapped pupils transferred to a mainstream class or to an empty classroom resulting from falling rolls. It cannot be overstressed that integration is no recipe for economy; viewed as such it is a strategy for disaster, involving the maximum neglect of those whose needs are greatest.

Predicting future needs is always hazardous, but based on current knowledge, it is possible to identify the likely priority areas or issues during the years ahead. Work and attitudes within the schools must surely head the list, with the recognition that while all children have widely differing aptitudes, gifts and temperaments and are in a sense special, the needs of some are more special than others. It will involve for each school the need to review periodically its aims and objectives, with a view to increasing its capacity to deal with learning difficulties, especially the moderate ones. As the 1981 Act, moreover, defines special needs as learning difficulties requiring educational facilities not generally provided in ordinary schools, there is ample scope and incentive for widening the provision to cater increasingly for some special needs, which should both reduce the burden of 'statementing' and also make some needs less obviously 'special'.

The task is clearly not solely a matter for the schools and their response to the highly complex and, for some, unfamiliar needs that confront them. It demands the involvement of the whole of the education service and a realization on the part of all that 'special education is everybody's business'.

In their deployment of teaching resources, the schools will need to maintain a balance between increasing specialist inputs and having due regard for the importance of good generalists and good subject teachers. Two contrasting dangers must be avoided: on the one hand the tendency to assume that every minor behaviour or learning problem must involve recourse to specialists, and on the other the excessive determination to cope and the rejection of much needed extra help lest it be seen as an admission of failure.

In-service training needs will continue to be of the utmost importance – school-based as well as through facilities supplied by LEAs and universities for specialists, senior teachers, heads and principals; and this must of necessity include the development of a general awareness of special needs for all teachers and not simply those who are more specifically involved. There will be an important contribution to be made by those special schools which continue to exist as centres of support and good practice for mainstream schools and as resources for teacher training, initial and in-service.

To operate effectively the schools should be at the centre of a network of partnerships; within the educational service collaborating with advisers, psychologists, welfare and careers guidance staff, and with related professionals from other services, especially medical and paramedical staff and social services departments. Close relationships and involvement with parents are of course crucial; and there should also be wherever possible involvement of the wider community. As with so many aspects of education, external influences and circumstances affect the process and its outcome, such as social and economic factors, the child's environment, the level of prosperity or deprivation in the community. Cooperation with voluntary agencies is important, for however good the public services may be, gaps will remain which they are well suited to fill; while there will be for them the ever present need to prod the public conscience and generate momentum for improvement.

The task of securing adequate funding will be far from easy; yet it is essential. We are all too often told that resources alone will not solve problems, and we are well aware of this; but it should not be inferred that resources are irrelevant. The requirements of the 1981 Act have substantial resource implications, while filling the gaps which remain, such as the needs of the under-fives and the post-sixteens, will require major increases in expenditure. In regard to the latter particularly, the deficiencies and under-funding are glaring – the absence of a coordinated national plan, the near-total dependence on extra resources provided outside the education service (notably the MSC), the chaotic diversity of wages, employment incentive payments, training grants, educational grants, special allowances, social security and unemployment benefits which should quickly be replaced by a rational and fair system of financial supports for the sixteen to nineteens. The bland assumption that extra costs can be met by eliminating waste, better management and financial control just will not do. Some scope for redeployment of resources may exist but this has its limits. Many LEAs, for example, are trying to save on costly residential placements by substituting their own day provision, which is entirely reasonable as long as those for whom a residential place is essential are not deprived of their only means of getting an adequate education.

Securing essential resources will involve a realistic assessment of expenditure both in regard to current programme needs and to future development plans. In the interests of continuity of policy and practice, a firm basis of agreement will need to be established between LEAs and central government. There is demonstrably a need for coherent national policies and for effective machinery for monitoring developments, identifying changing needs and making appropriate adjustments to policies and priorities after consultation with all the main interests involved. There is also a clear need to promote inter-professional cooperation within and beyond the education service and to provide the kind of leadership and opportunities for involvement that will be essential to keep morale high and sustain effort and commitment by many people over many years. Warnock recommended the establishment of a National Advisory Committee on Children with Special Needs with the task of advising government on 'the provision of educational services for children and young people with special needs and their coordination with other services'. Having regard particularly to the unevenness of standards and inequalities of opportunity, notably after school leaving age, it is important that combined efforts on the part of providers, voluntary bodies and parents should be made to secure implementation of this recommendation.

Notwithstanding continuing deficiencies in provision, the future prospects are not without hope. In the last decade or so, special education has been much more widely discussed and acknowledged as a key area of educational growth and development. There is increasing recognition across the whole service of the nature and spread of special educational needs and of their immense variety and complexity. There is too a real concern to do better within the 'mainstream' schools for children with mild or moderate difficulties – and indeed this is the essential corollary of current moves to achieve maximum integration of the more severely handicapped into the mainstream. Here too there is much ground for hope, provided (and only provided) that the forward drive is combined with a balanced judgement and an overriding concern for the best interests of each individual child.

Modern technology has already produced improvements and should be exploited further both to reduce handicaps and improve remedial measures. With continuing advances in medical skills, better pre- and post-natal care, the incidence of physical and sensory handicaps can be expected to decline. It has already happened with the elimination of polio, the reduction of deafness from rubella, and also with therapeutic abortions. Advances in technology are also contributing towards helping folk to cope better with the needs of ordinary life, particularly for example those with sensory handicaps. Changing attitudes are also important, including a less deterministic attitude to handicap, improved teaching methods and an awareness that performance can be improved through good teaching and training. The knowledge and skills are there and are growing. There is at present a fund of good will, compassion and interest, and a widely shared understanding of the need for and the direction of future progress. It must not be eroded through complacency or lack of resolve, but rather strengthened through continuing exploration and a sensitive awareness of what has yet to be achieved.

General Index

adult and community education, 101, 187
Adult Literacy and Basic Skills Unit, 101
Adult Day Centres, 117
Adult training centres, 99–101, 117
advanced level G.C.E., 94
advice, educational and professional, 15–19, 36–40
advisory staff, see LEA advisory staff in N. Ireland, 151
Advisory Committee for the Supply and Education of Teachers (ACSET), 128–9
Advisory Council on Education, (Scotland), 162
appeal committees
  clerk to, 73–5
  constitution and procedures, 19–20, 72–5
  Scottish, 165–6
appeals, 70–7
  against statements, 19, 46
  in Scotland, 164–5
  to courts, 76–7
  to Secretary of State, 20, 40, 52–3, 71–2, 75–6, 140–1
assessment, 8, 19–20, 28–69, 70–1
  aims of, 29
  formal, 14–16, 20, 31–41, 50, 71
  in different countries, 176–7
  informal, 29–30
  in N. Ireland, 154–5
  in Scotland, 164
  requests for, 49, 70
  units, (N. Ireland), 155
Australia, 2, 5, 173, 175, 181, 184
Australasia, 174, 182, 186
Autistic Society, 39

Bachelor of Education (B. Ed.), 128
  in N. Ireland, 156
Bangor (N. Ireland), 153
Belfast, 148, 152, 153, 159
Belfield Primary School, 135

Bellamy, T., 181, 186
Birmingham, 102
Blind, 3, 4
  provision in Scotland, 162
Boarding provision, 87, 88
  see also Residential schools,
  Out-county placements
  in N. Ireland, 155, 159
Bridgend College of Technology, 96
Burnham, 131, 154

Canada, 2, 5, 182
careers guidance and counselling, 97–8, 185
  careers teachers, 98
  careers officer, 139
Carlisle, M., Sec. of State, 10
Centre for Educational Research and Innovation (CERI), 173
Certificate of Education (FE), 132
Certificate of Pre-vocational Education (CPVE), 94
Certificate for Teachers of the Deaf, 130
Child Guidance Clinics, 16
Chronically Sick and Disabled Persons Act 1970, 14
Circulars
  2/75, 28, 55, 137
  1/83,
    Annex 1, 61–3
    and assessments, 16, 29, 36, 47, 50, 140–1,
    and collaboration, 122, 140–1
    and learning difficulties, 14
    and statements, 19
  3/83, 126
clinical medical officers, 111
closure of schools, 25
Coleraine (N. Ireland), 155
colleges of further education, see Further education
Committee on Special Educational Needs (COSPEN), (Scotland), 166–8

Community education, *see* adult and community education
Community health services, *see* health authorities
Community Homes with Education (CHE), 117
confidentiality, 38, 47–8, 114
Consultative Committe on the Curriculum, (Scotland), 166
Council for the Accreditation of Teacher Education (CATE), 125, 130
Council on Tribunals, 20, 75
Court Report, 30, 108–9
Cripples Institute, (N. Ireland), 153
curriculum,
  for integrated pupils, 80–82
  in N. Ireland, 151
  in Scotland, 166–8
  in other countries, 180–3, 186

Daniskole, 183
deaf, 3, 4, 129–30
  in N. Ireland, 153, 158
  in Scotland, 162, 169
Denmark, 183
Department of Economic Development (N. Ireland), 157, 158
Department of Education (DES), 10, 28, 92, 113, 121, 125
  Architects and Buildings Branch, 96
Department of Education for N. Ireland (DENI), 147, 149–51, 156–7
Department of Employment, 102
Department of Health and Social Security (DHSS), 99, 113, 121
Department of Health and Social Security (N. Ireland), 147, 157
diagnostic units, N. Ireland, 159
  see also Assessment Centres
Disabled Persons (Employment) Act 1944, 103
Downpatrick College, (N. Ireland), 158
Downs Syndrome, 85, 88, 129
Dyfed, 171
dyslexia, 14

Education Act 1981 (Commencement No. 2) Order 1983, 13
Education Acts
  (1921), 3
  (1944), 3, 4, 91–2, 134, 165
  (1946 – Scotland), 162
  (1947 – N. Ireland), 146, 153
  (1970), 4
  (1974 – Mentally Handicapped Children (Scotland)), 162

  (1980), 20, 72–4, 134, 171
  (1981 – Scotland), 162–3, 168
  (1981), 13–27
  and appeals, *see* Appeals
  and integration, 79–80, 82, 85, 87, 171
  and parents, 135, 139, 144
  and resources, 85, 191
  and voluntary bodies, 119
  assessment procedures, 28–9, 36
  effects of, 11, 57, 107–8, 114, 121
  passing of, 11
  transitional procedures, 48–9
Education and Library Boards (N. Ireland), 147–52, 154–9
educational guidance units (N. Ireland), 155
educationally subnormal (ESN), 4, 5, 78–9, 87, 128–9, 154–5, 159
  in N. Ireland, 154–5, 159
Education Order (N. Ireland), 146–7
educational psychologist, 15, 16, 36, 39, 41, 42, 44–5, 111, 137–8, 144, 145
  in N. Ireland, 151, 154
  in Scotland, 169
Education Welfare Service, 39, 145
employment 175, 181
  see also unemployment
European Economic Community (EEC), 2, 173–4, 183
Europe, Western, 5, 173, 174

Fallowfield Boys' School, Craigavon, 158
Federal Law, 94–142
  see Public Law 94/142
Feuerstein, Prof. R., 182
France, 178, 180–1
Further Education Unit, 133
Further Education, 91–105
  colleges, 22, 92–6
  colleges, N. Ireland, 156
  LEAs' statutory duty, 91–2
  training of FE teachers, 123, 131–2
  transition from school to, 22, 93, 95
  voluntary sector provision for, 119

Gateway clubs, 101
General Teaching Council (in Scotland), 170
Governors and Governing Bodies, 25, 134, 150
Granville Centre, Sydney, 184
Grunwald, L., 179
Gwynedd, 171–2

Hamilton, Sir J., 95

H.P. (Handicapped Pupils) forms, 28, 36
handicaps, 1, 4–5
   incidence of, 17–8, 80, 123
   provision in Social Service
      Depts., 117–8
Health and Social Services Boards (N.
   Ireland), 147–9, 159
Health Authorities and Health Service,
   and assessments, 15, 22, 23, 28, 30, 32,
      34, 35, 38, 55, 106–8, 110, 139, 158
   role of, and support provided by, 106–
      15, 116, 144
   statements and, 43
   structure of, 108–9
   transfer of duties to LEA, 4, 79, 86, 162
health visitors, 144
hearing impaired, 15, 82–3, 95
   see also partially deaf/hearing
Hereward College, Coventry, 94
Her Majesty's Inspectors (HMIs)
   and teacher training, 125, 131–2
   and Warnock Report, 10
   survey of primary education, 135
HMIs (Scotland)
   and curriculum, 168
   and national coordinating
      committee, 166
   report on learning difficulties, 163
Hester Adrian Centre, 100
Hobbs, Prof. N., 176–7
hospitals and hospital schools,
   in N. Ireland, 159
   in Scotland, 168

independent schools, 43, 85–6, 88
INSET, 131
Institutes for the Deaf and the Blind (N.
   Ireland), 153
Instrumental Enrichment, 182–3
integration and mainstreaming, 78–90
   and curriculum, 80–2
   see also curriculum
   definition and development, 2, 5, 8, 9,
      24–5, 27, 57, 82–6, 139, 189
   in countries overseas, 174–5, 177–80,
      185
   in N. Ireland, 154, 159
   in Scotland, 166
   of post-16s, 94
   value of, 89–90
intermediate treatment, 118
International Year of the Disabled 1981
IST, *see* teacher training
Italy, 177–8, 182, 185

Jaffe Centre, Belfast, 155, 158

Japan, 173
job opportunities, 103–4
Jordanhill College, (Scotland), 169
Jordanstown School, (N. Ireland), 159
Joseph, Sir K., Sec. of State, 28
Junior Occupation Centres
   (Scotland), 162
Junior Traning Centres 86

language problems, 13, 33
Local Education Authorities (LEAs)
   and assessments, 31–42, 55, 114, 139
   and closures, *see* closures
   and pupils' change of schools, 51
   and Social Services, 115–8
   and statements, 42–52, 55, 71–2
   and teacher training, 123–6, 131–3
   and the 1981 Education Act, 13–24
   appeals against decisions, *see* appeals
   duties of, 3–4, 14–15, 22, 24, 28, 57, 91–
      7, 120
   international visits of officers of, 174
LEA advisory staff, 125–6
link courses, 95
Londonderry, 152, 155

Madison, Wisconsin, 179
mainstream, *see* integration
maladjusted, 4, 5
Malcolm Sinclair Trust (N. Ireland), 153
Manchester University, 127, 129
Manchester Polytechnic, 127
Manpower Services Commission
   (MSC), 22, 101–3, 131, 133, 192
Maoris, 176
Medical officer, *see also* Health Authorities
   and assessments, 15, 16, 38
   role of, 16, 107, 111
medical examination, 41
Melville Report (Scotland), 162
MENCAP, 33, 91, 119, 120, 186
MIND, 33
Moray House (Scotland), 169
Muckamore Hospital (N. Ireland), 157
multiple handicap, 94, 189

named person, 22, 98, 121, 136, 138–9, 143
National Advisory Committee on Children
   with Special Needs, 11, 192
National Bureau for Handicapped
   Students, 133
National Council on the Training and
   Supply of Teachers, 128
National Health Service, *see also* Health
   Authorities
   and voluntary bodies, 120

involvement of, 106–8, 111–3
training of staff, 127
National Society for Deaf Children, 121
Newtownabbey School (N. Ireland), 159
New Zealand, 175, 176, 180
Non-maintained schools, use of, 43, 86, 87
North America, 173, 174, 186
see also Canada, U.S.
Northern Ireland, 146–162
Northern Ireland Polytechnic, 157
North Nottinghamshire College of FE, 96

Oregon, University of, 97, 186
Organisation of Economic Co-operation
and Development (OECD), 173–4,
177, 184
Oxfordshire, 79, 92

Parents
and appeals, 70–7
and assessments, 32, 33, 41, 49, 58–9,
70, 136–9, 141–3
and statements, 19, 43–6
and the 1981 Education Act, 14–21,
134–45
as partners, 31, 114, 124, 135–6, 141,
191
partially deaf/hearing, 4, 79, 83, 87
partially sighted, 4, 15, 82, 87, 170
peripatetic teachers, 22, 25, 42, 138, 145
in N. Ireland, 151, 154
PHAB clubs, 101
physically handicapped, 4, 82, 87, 94, 117
in N. Ireland, 154, 158–9
Portugal, 173, 177, 182
post-16s, 9, 22, 91–105, 170, 174, 183–5,
190, 192
pre-school children, 9, 13, 22–4, 41–2, 109,
111, 116, 139, 164, 190–1
psychiatric services, 40, 113
units, (N. Ireland), 159
psychologist, *see* educational psychologist
Public Law 94/142, 10, 57, 175, 179, 186
Puerto Ricans, 176

Queen Elizabeth's Training College,
Leathershead, 96
Queens University (N. Ireland), 156
Queen v. South Glamorgan Appeal
Committee, 76–7

reassessments, 21, 50
recorded pupils (Scotland), 164, 166
Regulations
Education (Special Educational Needs)
Regs., 1983, 13, 16, 35, 50–2, 74, 140

Special Educational Treatment
(Scotland) Regs., 1954, 163
Residential provision, 25, 46, 116–7,
192
see also Boarding provision
in N. Ireland, 155–6, 158

RNIB, 33, 120
RNID, 33
Rosstulla School (N. Ireland), 159
Routeways course (N. Ireland), 158
Royal Schools for the Deaf, 119
Rudolf Steiner, 95

Scandinavia, 175, 182, 183, 186
Schools Council, 57
committee for Wales, 172
Schools Psychological Service, 36, 97
Schroeder, 8, 179
Schwartz, 186
Scotland, 162–70
Scott, R. A., 176
Scottish Council for Research in
Education, 170
Scottish Health Education Group, 168
Secretary of State for Education and
Science
appeals to, *see* appeals
closure of schools, 25
criteria for teacher training
courses, 125, 129
Social Services Depts., 16, 28, 113,
115–8, 144
and ATCs, 99–100
and statements, 43
assessments, role in, 30, 32–5, 39, 55,
121
staff training courses, 127
Spain, 173, 177, 182
Spastics Society, 95
Special Educational Needs,
and the 1981 Education Act, 13–15
and Warnock, 9–10
identification of, 28–9, 121
incidence of, 17–18, 80–2, 123
see also handicaps
severe and complex, 81–2
statements of, 64–7
see also assessment, statements
Special Educational Needs Information
Exchange Project, 168
speech therapy, 111–2
N. Ireland, 159
Statements, 42–69
and the 1981 Education Act, 15, 17–
9

and under 2s, 23
form and preparation of, 42–3, 64–7,
    71, 140
in Scotland, 164
review of, 21, 51
see also reassessment
transfer to new LEA, 51
Sweden, 177, 180

teacher training, 9, 123–33
in service, 25, 88–9, 123–8, 130–2, 191
N. Ireland, 151, 156–7
Scotland, 169, 170
Technical and Vocational Education
    Initiative, (TVEI), 94
Thatcher, Mrs. M., Sec. of State, 6
Tizzard, J., 175
transitional provisions, 48–9

Ulster, University of, 156
United States, 2, 5, 10, 121, 173, 174–7,
    179–82, 186

Vanderbilt University, Tenessee, 176
Visual handicap, 95
    see also partially sighted

Voluntary bodies and organisations, 4,
    23, 87, 106–7, 118–21, 138–9, 144,
    191

Wales, 170–2
Warnock Committee and Report, 3, 6–
    11, 22, 26–7, 57–8, 163, 190
and assessments, 29–30, 58
and careers service, 98
and handicapped young people, 91–3,
    96, 100, 103–5
and integration, 8, 24, 78–9, 82, 171,
    189
and parents, 21, 135–8, 141, 144
and statements, 17
and teacher training, 128
and voluntary bodies, 118–9
Welsh Joint Education Committee, 170–2
Welsh language, 171–2
West Germany, 176

Young, Baroness, 10
Youth Training Scheme, 102, 157
Youth Training Programme (N.
    Ireland), 157–8
Yugoslavia, 173